FROM DEATH TO BREATH

FROM
DEATH
TO
BREATH

A Mother's Inspiring Story of
Resurrecting Faith and the *Power* of Miracles

KELLY MAUREEN

Published by Kelly Maureen

Hardback | ISBN: 979-8-9945733-0-3
Paperback | ISBN: 979-8-9945733-3-4
eBook | ISBN: 979-8-9945733-1-0

Scripture quotations marked NIV taken from The Holy Bible, New International Version® NIV® Copyright © 1973, 1978, 1984, 2011 by Biblica, Inc. Used with permission. All rights reserved worldwide.

Scripture quotations marked NKJV taken from the New King James Version®. Copyright © 1982 by Thomas Nelson. Used by permission. All rights reserved.

Scripture quotations marked AMP taken from the Amplified® Bible (AMP), Copyright © 2015 by The Lockman Foundation. Used by permission. www.Lockman.org

2nd Edition

For inquiries or to share your story, please contact:
Email: victory@kellymaureen.faith
Website: kellymaureen.faith

This book is dedicated to my resilient little *warrior*.

My dearest Vaughn, may you grow up knowing God's healing power that brought you back to us and we pray God continues the work He started in you the moment you were born.

CONTENTS

THE PREP

A PERSONAL PERSPECTIVE FROM THE AUTHOR'S HUSBAND

"...diligence is not immune to the unexpected, but with the power of prayer and faith, miracles do happen."

When we found out Kelly was pregnant, there was a lot of excitement and preparation. Personally, it took a few months for reality to really set in, particularly when I hung the six wooden blocks in the nursery that read, "VAUGHN." As a 38-year-old, pending new dad, I had a chance to witness numerous family, friends, and professional colleagues all open this chapter in their lives way before me. I took comfort in knowing "if they can do it, I can do it," but I'd be lying to you if I said there wasn't a part of me that was scared.

Thankfully, I had Kelly to guide and usher me through the process. Just like any other 21st-century first-time parents, we had our gender reveal party, hosted a shower, took the infant CPR class, joined in on some birthing classes, and purchased that oddly shaped pregnancy sleeping pillow.

However, Kelly's careful preparation was unparalleled; if there was a book about it, she was reading it, if there was a vitamin out there, she was taking it, and if there was a baby birthing YouTube channel, she was watching it. I applaud her for her studies and efforts to prepare her mind and body for birth, even though at times I admittedly thought they were above and beyond.

That being said, if any couple was ready for their son's birth, it was us! We were overprepared and went in with our perfect plan and strategy, but we quickly came out with the most powerful lesson of all: *diligence is not immune to the unexpected,* but with the power of prayer and faith, miracles do happen.

Kelly's proactivity in preparing for Vaughn reflects her commitment, love, and even her vulnerabilities, but those traits are what I believe helped her strengthen her relationship with God and push through the fear that followed Vaughn's birth.

This experience has positioned our family to face adversity more effectively, this time with a more realistic expectation, rooted in God's plan for perseverance and victory! Kelly's journey highlights some of her lowest emotional and spiritual moments, but the doubt and pain led her to find the faith and answers she needed for healing and restoration.

Through her commitment to and love for God, she wiped away the fear once and for all, making meaningful change in her everyday life for herself and us, her family.

It is my joy and hope that through Kelly's story, you can tap into the strength you need to wipe away any lingering spiritual, emotional, and/or relational fear to see the victory that God has for you.

And if you're praying for a miracle, may this book encourage your faith.

Thanks for reading,
Chris

THE AFTER

WRESTLING WITH FAITH & QUESTIONS

"*I have found that the significance in our story isn't just a happily ever after, but rather, for me, it's a story about what happens after.*"

Life is full of ups and downs. As a mother, you learn to deal with sudden surprises: runny noses, screaming fits, tearful moments, and even unexpected vomit. I have a new living room rug because of that last surprise. However, nothing can truly prepare you for the most unpredictable series of events: your child returning from the dead.

The phrase "Happily Ever After" frequently concludes the stories of fairy tales, indicating that what follows is far less thrilling than the tale itself. In our reality, "Happily Ever After" is merely a myth, as the most important events in my story unfolded after the miracle. In this journey of processing, I have found that the significance of this story isn't just a happily *ever* after, but rather, a story about the transformations that happened *after* my search for answers.

No one tells you what happens after you experience something you can't scientifically explain. No one tells you how to process something you are not physically and mentally wired to understand.

The discussion about the reality of miracles is not a recent phenomenon; in fact, it has been a central topic for thousands of years with some of the most gifted minds. This book is not my intent to conclude the debate, as countless individuals worldwide and throughout history have remarkable stories like the one you are about to read. Rather, my perspective concerns the journey of faith and healing that followed my experience of a real miracle. As far as I'm concerned, miracles are real and still happen today just like they did 2,000 years ago.

The day I started searching for answers to the miracle my family experienced marked the two-year anniversary of the event and my son, Vaughn's, big two-year-old birthday. He had just moved to his "big boy" bed, which gave him the opportunity to crawl out of his bed easily without the constraints of the crib railings.

Transitions like these bring their own set of worries to any mother. Will he be safe at night without the confining and safe rails of his crib? Will he understand the rules to stay in his room until morning? Will he be able to safely roll around in his larger bed without standing and jumping up and down on it? Clearly, I've read him the book, *Five Little Monkeys Jumping On The Bed*, one too many times, as it was causing me concern that this was going to become a reality.

The gravity of the significance of that day raised a mix of emotions; some were anxious and slightly upsetting, while others made me want to shout with joy as loudly as I could that my son was alive. But there's much more to the story; the fact that our boy is talking, running, and walking without assistance is the greatest mystery of my life.

Many mornings, I let my mind wander with big questions around what happened while daydreaming for answers, only to realize I put my son's cereal in the fridge and the milk in the pantry, and even worse, I microwaved my cellphone instead of my coffee. No one can give you the right instructions on how to tend to your mind like a gardener, perfectly weeding out the memories of pain and trauma so you can feel the gratitude and joy. Some days, I was left with overwhelming feelings of anxiety trying to process the significance of everything that had happened on my own.

You're probably wondering, if I witnessed a possible miracle, then how could there be anxiety and pain to follow? Shouldn't there be a limitless wave of gratitude, joy, and peace after receiving such an overwhelming gift like a miracle? While those are part of my experience, the event also supercharged my motherly intuition.

A mother's intuition can be seen as something that defies the natural laws of nature. Most mothers could share stories about how they were able to predict or prevent harm to their child through this magical instinctual hunch.

The day after my boy turned two, my husband, Chris, and I took Vaughn for a walk to our neighborhood park after dinner. Vaughn had a tantrum during dinner because he didn't want to eat the meal I had prepared; granted, I couldn't be too upset, as I knew it was a risk sneaking spinach into a sauce and calling it "dinosaur juice." A change of scenery after a 20-minute series of toddler tantrums was desperately needed for all of us.

We are very fortunate to live just a block from a large community park that features swings, slides, basketball and tennis courts, as well as a spacious football field and track. Vaughn's favorite activity was riding the baby and toddler swing, and he always ran to it first when we would arrive at the park. However, that day, Vaughn surprised us both by wanting to run around the empty field and chase his dad. I followed as a passerby. I pushed the stroller, and watched as they ran together, shouting, and dancing across the empty field. It wasn't long before something else captured Vaughn's two-year-old attention span.

"Wocks, daddy, wocks," Vaughn said as they veered off the field toward the sidewalk where he knew he could find a shiny new prized rock.

"Woa, big wock!" Vaughn shouted as he followed the sidewalk to the edge of the park, where a landscaper had beautifully lined the mulch edges with large mixed stones.

Vaughn's young mind knew that not even an expert rock collector like himself could dig out and lift those.

"Heaby, too heaby!" Vaughn pointed and exclaimed.

I noticed that Vaughn was crouching to look closer at the large quartz rock. I instinctively panicked, seeing in my mind that he was about to lean forward too far and fall face-first into the rocky mulch. My mind tried to reason, thinking that falling into a bed of mulch wouldn't be the worst way for a toddler to learn about gravity. However, I also saw there was a half-buried rock in his vicinity with a gleaming, sharp edge. I walked toward Chris to warn him of my intuition. But just before I reached them, Vaughn fell exactly as I saw in my mind, face-first into the mulch. Thankfully, he fell across the large rock, not directly onto it. He cried for me to come save him as his mouth was full of dirt and mulch. I hugged him, cleaned out his mouth, and tended to the left side of his face that was slightly scratched from the woodchips.

"This is exactly what I saw happening in my head; I told you I can predict the future!" I facetiously said to Chris as I picked the bits of wood chips off our son's clothing and hair.

Mother's intuition is a unique superpower that can effectively detect small dangers in exactly the right moments like that one. However, when a mother experiences maternal trauma, her intuition can become hypervigilant, creating a constant, heightened state that may lead to overprotective and heightened responses to what she perceives as danger.[1]

When Vaughn was five months old, I experienced a terrifying recurrence of spontaneous bouts of intense anxiety and terrifying thoughts as a result of this over-heightened intuition. I later discovered it was post-traumatic stress from experiencing a disturbing event with my child. After five months, enough time had passed for the shock of the experience to wear off, and the trauma was beginning to take hold. Chris and I were going through the motions as any parents would with a new baby, but I didn't realize the significance of what I was trying to process until I found myself with uncontrollable bouts of stress and fear.

One evening, after bathing Vaughn, I carried him over to the nursery to change him and get him ready for bed. I lathered him up with lotions and the latest chamomile- and lavender-scented baby tonics, then wrapped him in his blue quick-fastening swaddle. When I carried him back to our room to place him in the bassinet, I saw Chris cleaning our primary bathroom. He was vigorously wiping down the shower with standard bathroom cleaner you'd find in most homes. Any normal woman would be thrilled that their husband was cleaning and would want to cheer him on and thank him for his service to our family. But my mind did not assess the situation reasonably. I screamed as if I were in pain and he was a stranger going to kill my baby.

My mind immediately raced back to seeing Vaughn's lifeless body in the hospital. When I smelled the clean bathroom, the smell appeared to me like toxic green smoke escaping the bathroom to choke our sleeping baby boy. I was shaking and stunned with fear.

The questions that invaded my fragile mind at the time were too big for me to process. Would God punish me if we accidentally harmed the boy He saved? If Vaughn were back in the hospital, would he be saved a second time, or does he only get one miracle?

When you experience a traumatic event ending with an unexpected result, it isn't easy to understand how to stop your mind from racing back to the event or to try to make sense of the mystery as if you were solving a crime scene. If a crime scene warrants investigation, why shouldn't a suspected miracle also warrant one? Is it not also weighing the gravity of life and death?

During Vaughn's entire first year of life, I was living in this post-traumatic state, fearful of every sniffle and smell. I developed compulsive rituals I knew would keep my mind secure, like washing his bottles, pacifiers, and toys multiple times before I deemed that they were safe enough for my miracle child. I strived to keep the house as clean and sterile as possible. The cleaning and safety compulsive behavior kept me feeling he was physically safe, but it didn't help me get to the root of the pain: accurately processing *what* happened and *why* God saved my son.

I was constantly looking for signs that Vaughn was not normal, that there were lasting effects from everything he went through. I was hyper-sensitive to the growth charts from the pediatrician and the milestones of development, looking for proof that my son was not normal.

Despite my fears, Vaughn continued to meet and *exceed* all milestones.

He could point to certain animals in books when I asked before he was eight months old, which astounded his pediatrician. But the fact that my son crawled, walked, talked, and interacted on or ahead of schedule still wasn't enough proof for me to believe that he had experienced a true miracle. What made him so *special*?

More pressing questions regularly invaded my mind's ability to reason, causing intense anxiety. Would God bring my son back from the dead, but not completely heal him? Why does God choose to save some while others suffer? How rare was the event we experienced? If my son's life truly is the result of a miraculous intervention, then what does this mean for his life's purpose? Why is my baby alive when so many mothers have lost theirs?

You're probably reading this book because you are in one of two camps. The first camp is for those who believe in miracles, having either experienced one or looking for the hope and healing that faith in them can bring. The second camp is for those who are curious about the existence of modern miracles and are either looking for evidence of their occurrence or wish to read a story to discover explanations for these "unique events."

Before writing this book, I lived in both camps. One camp kept me safe and cozy by day, filling me with gratitude and hope for the future by believing in the miracle. The other camp ignited an unrelenting fire within me to seek answers for what really happened to my son. One camp led me to a sense of acceptance, and the other camp left me so thirsty for answers that I desperately searched for them.

Through my research, interviews, and significant spiritual reflection, I have found remarkable answers to my most critical questions that I can't keep to myself. This important quest has created opportunities for healing that might not have come without the effort of searching. My emotional and mental healing has been a beautiful outcome of this search. But there is an even more significant story to share, one that goes beyond just my journey. Whether you are a person of faith who believes in God or someone who does not believe in a higher power at all, reading the story of my son's unexpected healing and the answers I received for my spiritual and emotional healing will shake your faith to its core.

There were supernatural connections and experiences around my son's existence that not only led us to question more than just the miracle of the event itself, but see the divine power that was at work in our time of need every step of the way, while also paving the way for others who prayed over my son to receive their own miracle in their time of need.

We decided on the name Vaughn for our son when I was six months pregnant. After we sorted through the list of the 100 most popular boys' names, the name Harrison was our top choice. We teased the name to family and friends for a month or two, but it never really felt right. We ultimately decided to name him after Chris's dad, who had passed away in 2020 from complications of a severe heart attack and prolonged CPR. He was one of the kindest men I have ever met. He was only 66 years old and looking forward to his retirement, which was to begin just one week later.

In naming our son, we could never have imagined that he would inexplicably triumph over the same complications that his grandfather did not. Could this be another very unusual coincidence, or can miracles be the result of not just divine intervention, but also divine generational *redemption?*

We received reports from people who prayed for Vaughn, recalling visions during that time. One woman described seeing the exact room he was in at the hospital after praying, and others received prophetic dreams and visions we believe predicted the very day he would be healed.

Every time we share our unique stories of unexplainable divine intervention, we gain God's perspective on the puzzle of our existence and purpose. Is there an innate power in all of us that can tap into the miraculous power of supernatural healing, or is this something that only a few are capable of accessing? How powerful are prayer, hope, and faith, and what role did they play in my son's story? How does praying for others help us in our time of need?

Throughout history, humanity has told stories of moments that cannot be explained. Many Christians still believe today that through prayer, anything is possible, including bringing a person from death to breath.

This is my story.

Chapter Two

THE BEGINNING

AN UNEXPECTED BREATH

> *"Did our plea to God to save our boy bring him back to life?*

"It's now an emergency!" A new doctor with short blonde hair walked into the room.

I had been in labor for nearly 36 hours, and my baby was no longer descending. He shifted out of position, and his heart rate was dropping rapidly. What we had thought was a slightly complicated birth had turned into an emergency.

"I've been monitoring your baby's heart rate," the blonde doctor said, "and we now need to get him out as fast as possible, and I don't think you have the energy to keep going. There are two options: we can do an emergency C-section, or I can use the forceps and get him out now. Setting up for the C-section takes more time, which we may not have, but I can get him out in minutes with the forceps."

The new doctor squeezed my hand and reassured me that she was one of the most experienced with the device in delivery situations like these.

Chris and I agreed with the decision to get our baby out as quickly as possible. I was extremely exhausted and could hardly keep my eyes open.

A small team of nurses entered the room and stood along the side. "A precautionary measure," the doctor said.

She inserted the forceps and positioned herself. On my next contraction, my baby was out. They placed my baby's still body on my stomach while they waited for more blood flow from the umbilical cord. I was overwhelmed with exhaustion and emotion. Chris squeezed my hand as if saying, "You did it, Vaughn's here!"

The doctor began patting and wiping my baby dry to stimulate a response, but Vaughn remained unresponsive. The set of precautionary nurses came into action quickly when the doctor took my baby from my stomach before I could even see his face and handed him to them.

"Sometimes, babies need a little help," the doctor said, trying to reassure me not to panic. My midwife and doctor advised me to stay focused so I could be repaired from the physical damage caused by the rapid delivery.

Every time I blinked, it felt like minutes. Exhaustion and the shock of everything happening took over. Chris stayed by my side, holding my hand, looking panicked and nauseous.

All I could hear was the team of nurses around my son saying, "and one, and two, and three, and four, and five…" I would blink, and more time passed. "And one, and two, and three, and four, and five, and six, and seven, and eight, and nine…"

"What's happening?" I asked the doctor as I mentally drifted in and out. She calmly instructed me to focus and remain still.

Chris texted updates to my mother during this time. Vaughn was born at 5:18 in the morning, and the following text thread accounts for the timeline after his birth.

[5:44 AM] *Please pray for us*

[5:44 AM] *Baby not well*

[5:48 AM] *Please God*

When I looked around, the room was filling with people. Nurses were rushing in one after another. The small delivery room suddenly had twenty or more people surrounding my baby and us in the dark room. It was loud until suddenly, it was silent.

Everyone remained quiet, staring at Chris and then me. The chief doctor of the Neonatal Intensive Care Unit (NICU) slowly walked over and took a seat on a stool next to the delivery bed where I was lying, and Chris was standing. My right hand hadn't let go of Chris's hand for the past few hours. A young nurse gripped my left.

The doctor took a deep breath, paused, and then said in a very shaky voice, "I'm so sorry, we did everything we could, but your baby didn't make it."

I immediately looked up and screamed, "No God, no! Why God, why!?"

Chris bowed his head, and I could feel him shaking as our sweaty, stressed hands still held each other tightly.

I looked around the room at the somber faces and shadowy figures lining the walls of the still-dark room. Some looked down, others looked into my eyes with great sadness. I felt overwhelming terror and embarrassment simultaneously.

Shortly after that moment my mother received the texted news from Chris that our son didn't survive.

[5:54 AM] *Come now*

[5:54 AM] *We lost him*

"No, Jesus, No!" She, too, shouted out to God as I had in the delivery room. She writhed on the floor of our guest room while praying out loud with my dad, who had been talking to her on the phone when Chris's text came through.

Minutes later in the delivery room, a nurse shouted from the center of the room.

"We have a breath!"

The doctor quickly stood and headed to where my baby boy was lying motionless in the delivery room bassinet.

Did our plea to God to save our boy bring him *back to life*?

Chris updated my mom at 5:59 AM that Vaughn took a "possible breath," which was an astonishing 40 minutes after he was born.

Nurses hurried around the room while Chris and I were still recovering from the shock of the initial news.

A male nurse brought my tiny, blue, and still baby over to me. "Give him a kiss, Mama, quickly," he said.

I ungripped Chris's hand and gave my baby a quick kiss on the head, saying shakily yet sternly, "You fight, baby, you fight!"

The team of nurses ran with Vaughn to the NICU for emergency care and assessment. Chris followed while I was urged to remain still as they completed my surgery. A few minutes later, the lights came on in the room. I felt like I was in a trance, barely able to keep my eyes open.

Was what happened real, or was it a dream?

I've never experienced such an overwhelming mix of loss, pain, elation, relief, confusion, and fear all at once.

My mother came into the delivery room looking as if she had been crying. She was shaking slightly. She didn't know whether my baby was dead or alive, and she couldn't even recall how she arrived at the hospital. After she received the devastating news that our baby didn't make it, and after she prayed with my dad, she got in my car and started driving without knowing the direction.

Because she was from out of town and had just arrived the day before, she didn't know which hospital to drive to or where she was, but she arrived at the right place as if she had an innate instinct of where to go.

The doula who assisted with the delivery came in and reassured my mom that my baby was alive, in the NICU, and that her daughter was brave and a fighter.

In the NICU, Chris watched the medical team hook his son up to every device. IVs were being set up with narcotics for pain relief, medication, and sedation. Vaughn's heart and head were covered in monitoring devices, and his face was taken over by an intubation tube and mask.

A blue card was taped to the front of his hospital bassinet that read he was surprisingly nine pounds and four ounces. Certainly, not the expected size for a baby in the NICU.

Our baby was placed on an advanced cooling blanket. This cooling blanket dropped his body temperature to a hypothermia state between about 91.4°F to 93.2°F. This is a technology used in advanced NICUs to slow Hypoxic-Ischemic Encephalopathy (HIE), brain trauma, as a result of the extended lack of oxygen.[2] Even with this life-saving technological advancement, a significant number of infants who receive the cooling blanket treatment still do not survive or survive with neurodevelopmental disability.[3,4]

Chris returned to the delivery room, where I was with my mother and another nurse, still awaiting transfer to the recovery room.

"I was with our son; he's alive and hooked up to everything," said Chris, a little shaky and off balance.

The NICU doctor walked back into the delivery room and sat in the same chair where she had informed us of our boy's passing. I immediately prepared for more bad news as I held Chris's hand tightly.

"He's in the NICU and in critical condition." She paused. "In about 1 percent of births, babies need CPR. Your son, however, received a lot of CPR and 5 rounds of epinephrine."

She went on to explain that she does not usually deliver more than 3 rounds of epinephrine because, in her experience, it can do more harm than good. Our newborn son had to be given nearly double. In that moment, Chris and I understood the gravity of the situation. Our baby was alive, but his condition was critical, and his chance of survival — let alone a normal life — was low.

It is estimated that *less than* 0.1 percent of newborns require epinephrine during resuscitation at birth.[5] And when resuscitation extends beyond the first critical minutes, the likelihood of a full recovery becomes increasingly unlikely. According to Chris's texts, our baby could have received more than 30 minutes of CPR, and it was about 40 minutes before he took his first breath. We were facing a substantial possibility of mortality or severe neurological impairment.

She continued, "We've put him on a cooling blanket, which can help with the trauma to the brain, and have seen both good and poor outcomes. Children may have delayed walking or talking development or severe disabilities like cerebral palsy. We have no way of knowing how your son is going to do."

My mind immediately pictured a sick child in a wheelchair, and I thought about how impossibly difficult the life ahead of us would be if our child did survive. Was I mentally and emotionally strong enough to handle taking care of a child with intense disabilities? I began to feel the guilt that accompanied the overwhelming sense of pity for myself.

We had witnessed the impossible: our son was dead and now is alive! But we were far from celebration.

We realized that a positive outcome was becoming less likely as our baby suffered very serious injuries from the birth and the prolonged CPR. But after further research, we now believe our son may also have experienced the rare event known as *The Lazarus Phenomenon*.

The Lazarus Phenomenon, also known as the Lazarus Effect, is a rare event in which an individual declared dead suddenly shows signs of life after failed CPR, resembling a miraculous revival.[6]

To this day, the precise cause and mechanisms behind this

unexpected and spontaneous return of life remain unclear to medical professionals.[7] This medical term is named after the story of Lazarus in the Bible (John 11), who was raised from the dead after four days in his burial tomb.

The Lazarus Effect is an extremely rare phenomenon, with only a few dozen reports ever to be documented in the medical literature since it was first described in 1982.[6] Unfortunately, many individuals who experience this phenomenon do not survive for long after the event; severe complications from prolonged oxygen deprivation and trauma during CPR are more common.[6]

Pediatric instances of the Lazarus Effect are exceedingly rare; one review identified only four documented pediatric cases.[7] A newborn surviving, let alone experiencing the Lazarus Effect, may be extraordinary, as research points to the seriousness and rarity of prolonged CPR on infants.[8]

Chris wheeled me back to the mommy-and-baby wing. Entering what was supposed to be my first few days of bonding with my new baby boy became my lonely terror. I could hear the halls filled with crying babies and laughing new mommies as he wheeled me to our room. My stomach felt twisted and empty as I listened to a stranger's baby crying through the walls.

The staff's eyes seemed sad when they saw us making our way through the hospital wing. Nurses would stop and say, "We're praying for him." But it felt like empty pity cast into the ocean, where our hopes were sinking fast.

A few hours later, Chris and my mom wheeled me into the NICU to visit Vaughn for the first time, but I couldn't see his face. His body was blue, swollen, and full of tubes. His hands and feet were covered in IVs and tape, leaving barely any open space where I could touch his skin for the first time. I had to stand up to reach him, but the doctors said that because of my birth-related physical trauma, I couldn't. This formed a physical and mental barrier preventing me from interacting with my baby. All I could do was sit and listen to the beeps of the machines, helpless and desperately tired. No matter the outcome for my child, dead or alive, I prepared my mind to face a sad future.

After the first night in the NICU, Vaughn's status took a dark turn. We were told that his blood gas levels were not normal, and his complexion turned from slightly blue to white.

A nurse I had never seen before entered my recovery room to deliver me pain medication and asked how I was doing. I told her my baby was in serious trouble, and I wasn't sure if he was going to die that night. She grabbed my hand and held it for a long time that night while I cried; to this day, I can still remember the feeling of her comforting hands.

She didn't speak much to me other than showing me a piece of paper with her favorite Bible verses for strength to help me cope with the intense emotional pain of the moment. She even sat with me and allowed silence to fill the room for a time of peace as I read the verses she prepared for me until a phone call abruptly interrupted the moment. It was Chris calling from the NICU.

Our son was declining fast, and he was going to run through the halls to wheel me back to the NICU as quickly as possible as if he were racing against the time our son had left.

Sometimes I wonder if that gentle and quiet nurse was really a nurse who was making her rounds on assignment, or if she was on a more *divine* assignment preparing me to stay strong for what was about to happen. I don't remember ever seeing her again.

*Do not forget to show hospitality to strangers, for by
so doing some people have shown hospitality to angels
without knowing it.*
(Hebrews 13:2, NIV)

When we arrived back to the NICU, the doctor on call did not sugarcoat the situation and give us any hope. This doctor most likely viewed honesty as a form of kindness to families facing life-and-death situations.

"We will still do what we can, but your son has *a lot* of problems," she told us a few times very stoically. "We need your signatures to give him emergency blood transfusions and airlift him to a more equipped hospital. You need to know it is not looking good. He has more problems than we can handle here."

Looking back on how the doctor delivered the news, it was clear that we needed to know the truth of the situation. Our son was dying, and their NICU was not equipped to handle a complicated and rare case like Vaughn's.

The air crew arrived to prepare our baby for the journey. The pilot was a woman with long blonde hair pulled back. She looked just like my aunt. She approached us with gentleness as we signed papers in preparation for our baby's risky journey in the sky. I felt comforted in seeing her family resemblance.

"We will get him there safely, but we need to move quickly," she reassured us as she rolled the papers back into a red folder.

Chris pushed my wheelchair aside, where we had privacy to hug and cry together, believing it would be the last time we saw our baby boy.

It all didn't seem real. Vaughn now resembled something from an extraterrestrial movie, swollen and coated with a white, chalky substance. I watched as they lifted the white alien from its bassinet and placed it in what looked like a microwave, amid huge gray blocks carrying narcotics, medicine, and fluids for the journey. At that moment, I felt a sense of emotional separation. How could this pale creature be my baby?

"He looks scary," I repeated several times to Chris in shock.

After they raced this machine carrying our boy into the helicopter, the room felt heavy and thick. By now, we hadn't slept for nearly three days, and the physical and emotional pain was setting in. Although our boy came back from the dead, his chances of staying alive seemed very slim.

Did Vaughn just come back to die *again?*

THE MIRACLE

VICTORY FOR HEALING

> *"I believe in science, but there's something more happening with your son."*

After Vaughn was airlifted to a more advanced pediatric hospital on the East Coast, Chris and I requested an early discharge from our current hospital. Chris had to prepare the final paperwork and birth certificate, but paused because he didn't know if he was filling out papers for a baby that was going to live. While we were preparing to leave, the head doctor who had delivered Vaughn walked into my room.

I was surprised to see her in casual clothes. She told me it was her day off but she came in after hearing Vaughn had been medevacked and we were about to leave. Out of concern, she wanted to check on my healing progress before I left early.

"I have been trying to make sense of what happened to Vaughn in delivery," she started to say. "I consulted with some of the best doctors I know to put together a medical explanation, and some have a theory that his SA node in his heart did not kick start properly at birth."

She explained how our hearts are built to experience an electrical jolt at birth, and Vaughn's not only didn't start, but his backup node didn't start either; however, this was only a theory, and we may never know the true reason for his death-to-breath moment.

"I was thankful that I was focused on your surgery when everything was happening because it was a tough moment for everyone in the room. I believe in science, but there's something *more* happening with your son," she said alluding to a more divine involvement.

She hugged me as I cried and offered me advice on how to heal physically over the next few weeks. She said she'd call me for updates while checking with colleagues she knows at the hospital, where Vaughn was transferred.

After we were discharged that morning, Chris and his brother drove to the new hospital, about an hour's drive from our house. We agreed for me to stay home to get some much-needed rest. Parts of my right leg was numb, and I wasn't able to stand or walk.

My mom helped me into a hot bath for relief when we received a phone call from the overseeing cardiologist. Vaughn had just arrived and was assessed by the hospital's team of doctors, nurses, and specialists in the NICU.

"Vaughn may not survive, and you should prepare yourself. He is in very critical condition," the doctor explained on the call.

It was the call we dreaded. Prepare for the worst.

The medical team reported that post the cardiac arrest and pulmonary hemorrhage, Vaughn had wide-complex tachycardia. His heart was in trouble and not pumping blood correctly. We suspect it was the after-trauma of extensive CPR. At this point, he was still on the cooling blanket for his brain, but they needed to tackle the most immediate trauma first—his heart.

They were preparing the Extracorporeal Membrane Oxygenation machine (ECMO), an advanced life support device that takes the blood out of the body, oxygenates it, and then pumps it back in. This machine is rarely used on newborns and is reserved for only the most critically ill infants, since respiratory failure in newborns is uncommon for NICU admissions, and only a small number of these infants would ever need risky and advanced interventions like the ECMO.[9,10]

While some infants do survive, the sad reality is that studies show that after ECMO, children may suffer from a variety of disabilities, and it is an area of current research.[11]

Chris and I were very familiar with the ECMO machine because my father-in-law was on it after extended CPR just before he passed away a few years earlier. Hearing this news while en route to the hospital intensified Chris's anxiety as it reminded him of the trauma he lived through when his father had passed.

After I heard the news of the poor diagnosis and plan for ECMO, I felt a sense of emptiness. I stared at my toes in the bath water as I felt the bottom of the bathtub fall away. I was now floating aimlessly in the vast ocean with no direction or view of the shore. I was drowning in a numb feeling from my head to my toes. I thought of my baby's face as a toddler, then a teenager, and then as an adult. I saw the entire life I hoped and wished for him in a matter of minutes.

It was as if I was thinking to myself, *I don't even know you, how can I love you so much?*

About an hour later, when Chris and his brother arrived at the hospital, they learned that Vaughn no longer needed the ECMO machine because the condition of his heart and oxygen had started to improve unexpectedly.

He was now stable. How did a newborn who we thought was about to die just become *stable*?

Was this another divine intervention?

After hearing the news, I remember praying to God. Suddenly, I allowed myself to see those future visions of my son a bit more clearly in my mind. At that moment, I refused to give in to the pity party I was having for myself and I changed my thinking to the idea that my son had a chance to be well.

A day earlier, Chris presented me with a gift he had planned to give me in celebration of Vaughn's birth —a beautiful rose gold necklace with a "V" in the center, covered in small crystals. I wore this necklace every day Vaughn was in the hospital because it became a visual reminder in support of his healing, and at some point, it was no longer just "V" for *Vaughn* but also "V" for his *victory.*

After determining that Vaughn's heart was the biggest concern, the doctors transferred him to the Cardiac Intensive Care Unit (CICU) for treatment. That evening, Chris stayed the night in Vaughn's room while I stayed home for additional rest and healing. Vaughn was intubated and still on the cooling blanket. They had put a non-invasive small pacemaker from the 1950s on him, which helped maintain a steady heart pulse without any heart surgery, and he remained stable that entire first night in the CICU.

Many doctors looked over Vaughn's condition in the CICU. Some were fellows and others were cardiac surgeons. But the chief cardiac doctor of the floor said something to Chris and his brother when they arrived at the hospital that Chris will never forget. The chief cardiac doctor said that Vaughn was an absolutely "fascinating, just fascinating case."

In fact, the doctor was *fascinated* how Vaughn went from A to B to C. That is, A, being pronounced deceased after prolonged CPR and surviving; to B, alive but medevacked to their unit and requiring serious interventions for survival; to C, unexpectedly improving and now in a monitoring and managing state without risky interventions like ECMO.

The next morning, I was excited to see my baby, a feeling I hadn't experienced before. Chris drove back home in the morning to pick me up and go to the new hospital with him. He wheeled me through to the CICU floor of the hospital, where I saw a large glass room with a little bassinet in the middle of the room surrounded by towering medical devices and machines. On the door was a nametag: Vaughn.

"Is that the mother?" I heard the three nurses whisper as I was rolled up to the entrance of the room.

I suspected that Vaughn was being discussed as a strange medical case, and I could sense the news of his condition traveling throughout the entire third floor. When I saw Vaughn again, the only way to describe the emotion was like water flowing through my legs first and then up and out through my eyes.

"My baby," I whispered to him as I touched his device-covered head with tears running down my face. "My beautiful boy, I love you. Don't worry, you're going to be OK."

There was brown stuff coming out of his intubation tube which meant his lungs were still draining and recovering from some internal bleeding. Boxes of medicine and narcotics were stacked on the right side, and tanks of oxygen and other gases lined the entire back of the hospital bassinet.

He had IVs and devices in so many places, which is very shocking view to see on anyone, let alone on a newborn baby.

But even after seeing all of that, I still saw and hoped in the end vision I had for him. Victory.

You'd probably think I was delusional after seeing everything going on in that room, but I had peace along with the pain.

I started a group text with a few of my closest friends around this time. These friends were strong in their faith, and I asked them to become my small "circle of prayer warriors." I was selective about sharing the news because I had just gone from drowning in feelings of hopelessness and self-pity to filling up my heart tank and mind with hope. I wanted those close to me to have a strong mindset in this situation. I briefed them on everything we'd been through and on Vaughn's condition. I ended with:

I'm still clinging to the hope of bringing home my baby boy soon.

One of my friends told me two years later that when she shared the news with her family of what was happening with my son, they told her to prepare to console a grieving friend. But she chose to remain in prayer with a miracle in mind.

That afternoon, my dad and mom joined us at the hospital to visit Vaughn. Because of his critical condition, only a maximum of two people were allowed to enter Vaughn's room. I stayed in the room, while Chris shifted in and out. My dad came in, placed his hands on Vaughn's head, and I saw him start to cry.

"Don't cry, Dad, he's going to be ok," I instinctively said.

"I know. I know," my dad reassured me.

It's challenging to think of a moment when I saw my dad cry. He is a very passionate person. But his default is excitement, not sorrow. He later told me he was praying over Vaughn when he was crying.

Over the next 24 hours, there were pivotal moments for Vaughn. They needed to warm his body back up slowly and safely, and they didn't know what to expect. Studies show that newborns treated with the cooling blanket for HIE have a significantly higher incidence of seizures during the rewarming phase than during cooling, and these seizures are associated with an increased risk of death or moderate to severe disability.[12]

Chris and I decided to make short-term accommodations close to the hospital. I don't know how we were able to sleep that night, but by the grace of God, we had peace. Vaughn's body rewarmed without any issues, and he was awake for the first time.

The same chief cardiac doctor came to speak with us privately the next day. He suggested we make arrangements to stay closer to the hospital for a long-term period. His professional opinion was that we may be there for months and mentioned that some families stayed for a year or longer. No one had any idea how long Vaughn would remain in the CICU, and we needed to prepare for the long journey ahead.

I don't remember if it was this same day or another, but this doctor was always very encouraging to me and he asked why I wore the same necklace every day and if it held any significance to me. I remember telling him that it was a gift from Chris for Vaughn's birth, and that I was wearing it in support of Vaughn's victory. I'm sure he was encouraged by my answer.

In that moment, I just thought he was a little more observant and curious than most people to ask such a random personal question. But in hindsight, it was a very strange thing to ask a new mother in those circumstances. I now believe it was something that God prompted him to ask because it forced me to answer out loud what we were already believing in our hearts: God's victory over Vaughn's life.

Over the next few days, Vaughn continued to heal quickly. After just one week in the CICU, his heart, lungs, and blood recovered. In just a few days, not months, not one year, my son was well!

While the team of doctors made arrangements for Vaughn to be transported out of the CICU and to the NICU, to wean him off of the last bit of oxygen, and to teach him how to feed, one of the cardiac doctors monitoring Vaughn stayed behind to speak with us. He was a very tall, kind, yet serious man who looked like he had something important to say, but he didn't quite know how to say it.

"You don't understand," he started.

"Your son was the most dire and sickest child on all the floors of this hospital. And in just one week, he is the healthiest. This is *not* normal," he said as if in shock.

I looked at him and said, "Of course, it's a miracle!"

The nurses were always cheerful when caring for Vaughn, and we had uplifting conversations with them, even sharing a few laughs during the days he was in the CICU. But after hearing the expression of disbelief from one of the primary doctors caring for Vaughn, I wonder how many of them genuinely believed that he would be okay and that we would see Vaughn's victory. Even upon Vaughn's arrival, we overheard nurses speak that Vaughn was the sickest child in the hospital.

Chris and I have a great deal of gratitude and love for all the caregivers who oversaw Vaughn during that time. Even if they feared for us, they chose to rise above it and display hope every moment in our presence.

When Vaughn was settled in his new room in the NICU, Chris and I felt like we had just conquered the world and we were so close to taking our baby home. That is, until we were reminded that there was still one huge hurdle in front of us: Vaughn's brain.

We were so thrilled that his heart and lungs healed miraculously quickly that we forgot he had been without oxygen for about 40 minutes at birth. As we were informed after Vaughn was born, severe oxygen deprivation at birth (HIE) is associated with high rates of serious neurodevelopmental disability, including cerebral palsy.[13]

Now that he was out of the CICU, Vaughn could have his brain scanned for the first time to detect any signs of abnormal brain activity. We would finally be confronted with this beast that had been lurking in the back of our minds since our son was born.

I would be lying if I said this didn't wreck us emotionally, but my mother reminded me every day that we were in the hospital to not worry, because God doesn't do half miracles: *the best was yet to come.*

While waiting for the MRI to be scheduled, Chris and I held and fed Vaughn for the first time. I did hold Vaughn once in the CICU, but he had so many tubes and devices covering him that nurses had to assist every moment. It felt intimidating, highly uncomfortable, and unnatural. It was a truly special moment for us to finally have our beautiful and resilient little warrior in our arms, free from so many medical restraints.

Chris said that "everything just felt right" when he saw me holding Vaughn in the NICU. The nurses were so excited when he drank his first full bottle that they asked us to save it as a keepsake. We didn't, because we felt that simply bringing our son home healthy was the only keepsake we needed.

Chris began a journal of short letters that he wanted to read to Vaughn when he was older. Here's an excerpt to provide some of his perspective during that time:

> *From day one, you have been remarkable, my little champion! Even all the doctors have said it's truly a miracle how you have rebounded, and we are on the home stretch to bringing you home! You're only eleven days old, but you have already taught me how to be a true fighter, how to stay strong, and to stay positive in the toughest of times. I can't wait to get to know you better, learn with you, and see you succeed and be happy in life.*
>
> *Love, Dad.*

The day of Vaughn's MRI, we learned that it was completely clean and we were sharing Vaughn's final *victory*!

After Vaughn was eating normally and free of any medical devices and oxygen, he was moved to a standard recovery room. When we reached the top recovery floor with Vaughn, the nurses there were eager to meet the "miracle" baby. They couldn't believe they were witnessing a now healthy baby boy with an APGAR score of 0 at birth, the score that meant no detectable signs of life.

Vaughn was so healthy when he reached the recovery room that they barely checked on him during the short time we were there.

After Vaughn was finally home, we began to hear reports from family and friends about specific prayers and spiritual visions that had occurred to them while Vaughn was in the hospital.

It wasn't until two years later that I had the courage and desire to pull back the curtain and peek at the prayer activity during the time of Vaughn's healing. What I found not only answered some of my deepest spiritual questions but also led me down a path of faith I've never gone before. I dove into very deep spiritual waters, and I started swimming in places in my relationship with God that I didn't even know existed. I found that the timing of pivotal moments in Vaughn's healing during those days directly correlated with what was said in prayer.

What I share with you in the following chapters are the revelations God gave me as I drew closer to Him and sought His answers to all my pressing questions about my son's miraculous healing.

These answers have profoundly impacted my life, mind, and perspective of God forever, as well as healed my post-traumatic stress, anxiety, and fear. Dear reader, if you are unsure about the power of prayer, the role of faith, and God's power working miracles today, keep reading.

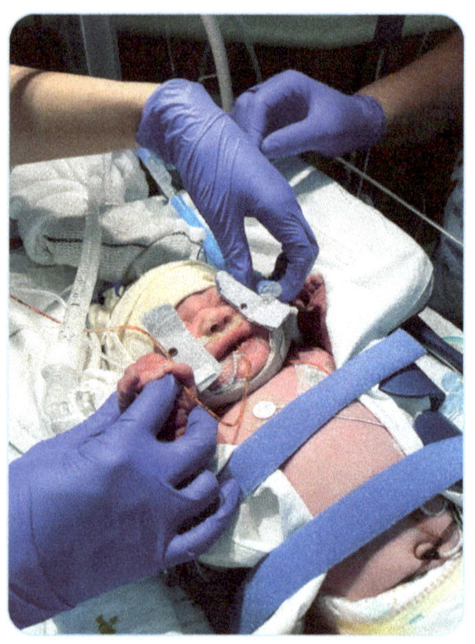

Picture of Vaughn arriving to the NICU after birth.

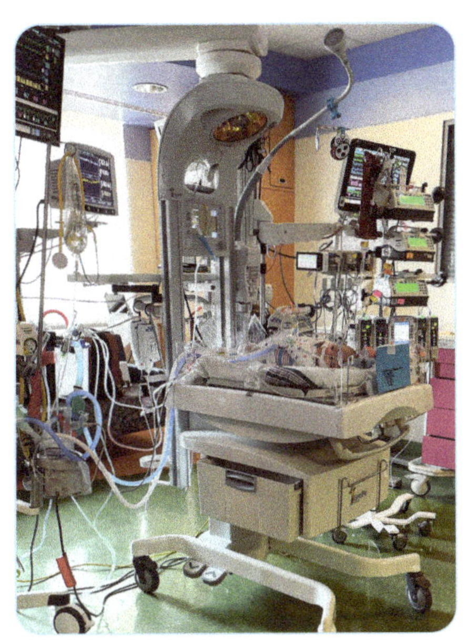

MAY 24, 2023

Picture of Vaughn in the CICU.

Kelly holding Vaughn shortly after he turned two years old.

Chapter Four

THE PRAYER

BEHIND THE HEALING

"When I took a closer look at the prayers, I saw the army battling alongside me, praying God's victory in faith with me before we saw it."

Chris called me to say he would be home late from work, and we should eat dinner without him. There had been a lot of political protests for months in early 2025, and protesters would stand on the bridges with signs to slow traffic. This added extra time to Chris's work commute. I was disappointed those nights, as political protests ruined our family meals together.

Vaughn and I quickly established a new routine of just the two of us at the dinner table, with me asking him questions to expand his vocabulary. One evening, I decided to focus my questions on understanding what Vaughn knew spiritually.

I asked, "Do you know who Jesus is?"

"Yeah," Vaughn said quickly, his mouth full of noodles.

"You do? Who is He?" I braced for a perfect two-year-old response, like "monkey" or "Elmo."

"He's daddy," Vaughn replied.

This made me pause eating and put my fork down. I asked again, "You think He's daddy?"

"Yeah, daddy!" He replied, very sure of himself. I was surprised, but I thought perhaps he overheard me praying once, saying "Heavenly Father," and made the connection on his own. So I asked him something I was sure he wouldn't know.

Then I asked, "Do you know what angels are?"

"Yes!" Vaughn replied even more emphatically than the first answer.

This was not enough to convince me. I paused a few minutes. Then, I remembered the specific prayers around angels and a vision that my mother had while praying for Vaughn when he was in the hospital. So, when he finished his meal, I searched on my phone for an illustration depicting the story of Jacob's dream from the book of Genesis.

The illustration depicted a man from the Bible, Jacob, sleeping while angels descended a staircase from heaven to where he lay.

I showed the illustration to Vaughn. Without me describing anything in the picture, he pointed at the figures in the painting and said, "Angels, Mommy, angels!"

I had never shown him a picture of angels before, nor had I explained what they are. At two-years-old, he had pointed to something, as if he recognized it, and confirmed it with me, just as he did with any other object he saw in real life that he recognized.

If you have a two-year-old, you know how amazing this is. Sometimes you will read a book twenty times, pointing out objects before they start accurately pointing out things on their own. I said the word "angels" once at the start of his meal, then later showed him a picture he had never seen before. He accurately pointed out the angels without any direction.

When Chris came home, I told him what our son had said, and he believed our boy knew heaven, too. Even if we learn that Vaughn didn't truly recognize angels or understand my questions about Jesus that night, we are convinced that God comforted him in his time of need.

When researching the events surrounding my son's miraculous healing, I had so many written prayers from people during that time as physical proof of the actual words prayed. This gave me a starting point for my research into the evidence I needed to reveal God's hand in my son's healing and understand what took place during prayer.

Before analyzing the specific prayers over Vaughn, I revisited the basics to gain a deeper understanding of what prayer is and how it works.

Is anyone among you suffering? Let him pray.
(James 5:13, NKJV)

UNDERSTANDING PRAYER

The Bible depicts prayer as various forms of communication with God. Whenever we speak, acknowledge, praise, or communicate with God, that is prayer at its most basic understanding. The Apostle Paul instructs in 1 Timothy that there are specific types of prayers we should be speaking.

I urge, then, first of all, that petitions, prayers,
intercession and thanksgiving be made for all people.
(1 Timothy 2:1, NIV)

It might be confusing that in Paul's definition of the types of prayers, he uses the word "prayers" as one of the categories. To clarify this, I examined the original Greek to understand his meaning. The original Greek word for "prayers" in this verse was *proseuchai*, the plural form of a general term for direct communication addressed to God.[14] So now we can accurately see that Paul is directing us with four very distinct types of prayer:

1 **Prayers of requests–**
asking God for something specific

2 **General prayers–**
communication addressed directly to God

3 **Prayers of intercession–**
praying on behalf of others and their needs

4 **Prayers of thanksgiving–**
thanking God for what He has done and will do

We also have a clear direction that our specific requests, or supplications, are to go hand-in-hand with thanksgiving. Or, more simply put, Scripture directs us to ask God for something with gratitude.

Do not be anxious or worried about anything, but in everything [every circumstance and situation] **by prayer and petition with thanksgiving,** *continue to make your [specific] requests known to God.*
(Philippians 4:6, AMP, emphasis added)

Seeing that gratitude and request were directed in the Bible to go hand-in-hand with our prayers was eye-opening. It stood out to me in this Philippians verse that God asks us *not to worry* about our needs and situation, and instead to pray with gratitude. Why would God direct us to exchange our worry for prayer unless that did something to change our situation? God is the same yesterday, today, and tomorrow (Hebrews 13:8). If He called us to exchange our worry for faith in Him, that is still true for prayer today. I saw a teeter-totter in my mind, with one end labeled *request* and the other *gratitude*. Each side is balanced by the other.

I came to understand that the reason this balance in prayer exists is that it is the catalyst of faith.

I now believe that I cannot have faith and ask God for something that I don't think He can deliver. I suspect this is why Paul directed that gratitude should always accompany our requests. Thanking God for what we ask at the time we ask takes considerable faith, as the answer is not yet seen but we trust in Him. It is comforting to know that God already knows our needs before we ask them (Matthew 6:8).

*And the **prayer offered in faith** will make the sick person well; the Lord will raise them up.*
(James 5:15, NKJV, emphasis added)

Not only does it take faith to be grateful to God before your prayer is answered, but it takes faith to believe that you *will* see it answered because you know God is capable even when it's answered in *His* way.

*"And whatever things you ask in prayer, believing, you
will receive."*
(Matthew 21:22, NKJV)

*"It shall also come to pass that before they call, I will
answer; and while they are still speaking, I will hear."*
(Isaiah 65:24, NKJV)

The written prayers I received, asking for Vaughn's miraculous healing, not only thanked God for Vaughn's healing before we saw it, but they thanked God for who He is because we had faith to see it. These, in my opinion, were the prayers of faith. In addition to gratitude, prayers over Vaughn were always aligned with Scripture. I began to see that using God's Word in prayer is a God-given tool to direct and build our faith. Many verses emphasize the importance of using God's Word in prayer for healing. Here are just a few:

*My son, pay attention to what I say; turn your ear to
my words. Do not let them out of your sight, keep them
within your heart;* **for they are life to those who find
them and health to one's whole body.**
(Proverbs 4:20-22, NIV, emphasis added)

He sent out his word and healed them; *he rescued them
from the grave.*
(Psalm 107:20, NIV, emphasis added)

Do not be wise in your own eyes; fear the Lord and shun evil. **This will bring health to your body and nourishment to your bones.**
(Proverbs 3:7-8, NIV, emphasis added)

For the word of God is **alive and active.** *Sharper than any double-edged sword...*
(Hebrews 4:12, NIV, emphasis added)

God's Word was very much present in the written prayers I received, whether summarized or quoted directly. Scripture was used as a declaration of praise, power, and reinforcement over Vaughn's healing.

DIRECTLY ANSWERED PRAYERS

To my surprise, some of the prayers matched the timing of what happened during Vaughn's healing. Chris kept a diary over the days Vaughn was in the NICU, and he wrote a few entries summarizing important moments that happened. We also took detailed photos of the events at the time, allowing me to review the dated prayers and see that some requests were directly answered on the same day or shortly after they were written.

My mother has kept a written journal of her prayers for decades. Every morning, she writes out her prayers and praises, and when Vaughn was in the hospital, this was no different. When Vaughn first arrived at the CICU, she wrote about the story of Hagar in Genesis. Abraham sent away Hagar, his servant, and her young son Ishmael because his wife Sarah didn't want Ishmael to compete with the inheritance of their son Isaac, as both were sons of Abraham. Abraham sent them away in the wilderness with food and water, but when the water ran out, Hagar placed her young son under a bush and walked away because she could not stand to see her child die.

"...I cannot watch the boy die." And as she sat there, she began to sob. God heard the boy crying, and the angel of God called to Hagar from heaven and said to her, "What is the matter, Hagar? Do not be afraid; God has heard the boy crying as he lies there. Lift the boy up and take him by the hand, for I will make him into a great nation." Then God opened her eyes and she saw a well of water. So she went and filled the skin with water and gave the boy a drink.
(Genesis 21:16-19, NIV)

From my mother's journal:

"You hear the cries of Vaughn, Father, up into heaven – I pray he will be mighty for your Kingdom. Kelly will be able to take him by the hand and bring him home. God was with the boy (Ishmael) as he grew up. God gave him a drink – today Vaughn will get a drink."

Looking back at the timeline, we believe that around the time of this prayer, Vaughn started receiving my milk and formula through a feeding tube, and he drank milk through a bottle just six days later.

Another prayer was answered on May 28, 2023:

"Father, complete your healing for Vaughn– may he breathe on his own and have no scar tissue in his airway or lungs. His brain will be perfect because you touched this child and you gave him breath. Thank you for your healing, you are able and you are willing. You bring life and protection to our family."

That same day, the doctors were weaning Vaughn's oxygen support, and he was breathing mostly on his own for the first time. The next day, Vaughn had his MRI, and we learned that he was neurologically healed. The timing of that prayer aligned with the healing.

THE PRAYERS OF AGREEMENT

I also found many duplicate prayers, which led me to search for prayers that were in *agreement* with each other.

---

*"Again I say to you that **if two of you agree** on earth concerning anything that they ask, it will be done for them by My Father in heaven."*
(Matthew 18:19-20, NKJV, emphasis added)

I shared earlier that I wore a necklace with a "V" to represent my faith in God's victory for Vaughn's healing while he was in the hospital. To my surprise, I found numerous prayers that highlighted the word "victory." When I took a closer look at the prayers, I saw the army battling alongside me, praying God's victory in faith *with me* before we saw it.

Here are just a few of the shared prayers speaking the same theme of victory:

*"[Vaughn] would be unharmed and tread in **victory** upon the lions and the cobras."*

*"[Vaughn's] **victory** is already won through the finished work on the cross."*

*"Win this battle, [Vaughn is] **victorious** in our God."*

About a month after Vaughn was home from the hospital, I received in the mail a picture from a woman I had never met. It was a small, hand-drawn, colored pencil picture of two figures holding up a small child in the sunlight. It looked as if they were on a shore because the area behind the figures was colored like water. On the picture was handwritten the words, "As God parted the Red Sea and the Jordan for his people to cross over to the Promised Land… so you are being carried across on dry land to the other side in *victory*, safely delivered."

When I opened this letter again two years later, I started crying because I never noticed when the woman had dated it. At the bottom, in small numbers, it reads "5/29/23." This was the day we celebrated that Vaughn's oxygen support had been fully lowered. It was also the day he had his MRI—the moment we were able to claim *victory* over our son's healing for the first time.

We believe Vaughn was indeed delivered from his battle that very day the woman drew the picture.

I thought it was interesting that she noted the two miraculous crossings for the Israelites: God performing miracles to lead them across the Red Sea to deliver them from slavery to the Egyptians (Exodus 14) and then again leading them across the Jordan River on dry ground into the Promised Land. But the second time, leading them across the Jordan was a miracle that marked the fulfillment of God's promise. This stood out to me because it parallels Vaughn's healing; he was also delivered twice. The first time was at birth when he took an unexpected breath after he was pronounced dead, and the second time was when he received expedited healing for his heart, lungs, and brain less than two weeks later.

I now view Vaughn's second healing as God's fulfillment of His promise, when He gave him breath, just as He did when He miraculously delivered His people a second time across the Jordan River and into the Promised Land.

I believe that God was giving many of us praying over Vaughn the same word, *victory*, because He had already won the battle for Vaughn's life, and we were praying to enforce it in agreement of our faith, even if we were praying thousands of miles apart.

Another prayer of agreement I found was the visual of God covering Vaughn.

"Cover Vaughn with your whole body over him and renew and restore every organ and neurological capacity."

"God, we thank you for stretching yourself across his body, bringing his body into alignment with yours."

There are multiple stories where this idea is matched in the Bible. The first was in 1 Kings 17, when the prophet Elijah stretched himself out three times over a dead boy, and the boy came back to life. The second instance is found in 2 Kings 4, where the prophet Elisha (Elijah's successor) stretched himself over a boy twice, from head to toe, after he prayed, and the boy came back to life.

*When Elisha came into the house, the child was dead and lying on his bed. So he went in, shut the door behind the two of them, **and prayed** to the Lord. Then he went up and lay on the child and put his mouth on his mouth, his eyes on his eyes, and his hands on his hands. **And as he stretched himself out on him and held him, the boy's skin became warm.** Then he returned and walked in the house once back and forth, and went up **[again]** and stretched himself out on him; and the boy sneezed seven times and he opened his eyes.*
(*2 Kings 4:32-35, NIV, emphasis added*)

I found it interesting that, in both of these stories, the boys didn't come back to life after a single attempt. It took a persistence of faith. Vaughn's healing was also a persistence of faith and prayer.

The third story of reference from the Bible is in Acts 20, when the Apostle Paul threw himself over the young man after he died, falling from a three-story window. Paul had so much faith after he hugged the young man who had died that he said, "Do not be troubled, because he is alive." Then Paul went back into the house to eat and continue preaching to the crowd in the upper room, and miraculously they took the boy home alive.

VISIONS AND PROPHECY

The Bible often records God speaking to people through visions and dreams. These visions and dreams were confirming God's promises or speaking of what's to come—a word of prophecy.

Many people shared prophetic visions and words they received about Vaughn while praying during the days he was in the hospital. I found one particular prayer for Vaughn to remember his healing, and that his memories of everything God spoke to him while he was in the hospital would never fade.

There were many requests for angels to comfort and protect Vaughn. Here are just a few of the written verses about angels that were highlighted in prayers I received for Vaughn:

For he will command his angels concerning you to guard you in all your ways; they will lift you up in their hands, so that you will not strike your foot against a stone.
(Psalm 91: 11-12, NIV)

Are not all angels ministering spirits sent to serve those who will inherit salvation?
(Hebrews 1:14, NIV)

The angel of the Lord encamps around those who fear him, and he delivers them.
(Psalm 34:7, NIV)

And, here are a few of the prayers I received that mention angels:

"Let your angels speak to Vaughn, "Do not be afraid."

"You command angels to minister to our baby Vaughn, and because we love you, no harm will come near our home, our children, and our children's children."

"Hope is here. Jesus is here. His angels surround Vaughn."

My mother had a very vivid vision while praying for Vaughn in the hospital. Above his plastic incubator and oxygen tubes, she saw angels descending and ascending on a staircase to comfort him from heaven. Right after she had the waking vision, she received a text from an unknown number, someone who was praying for Vaughn, but she didn't know them personally. The text said that angels were ministering to and comforting Vaughn at that very moment.

How could the person have known that my mother was having visions of angels comforting Vaughn at the *same time*? In her journal, my mother wrote that the vision was like Jacob's ladder.

He had a dream in which he saw a stairway resting on the earth, with its top reaching to heaven, and the angels of God were ascending and descending on it.
(Genesis 28:12, NIV)

After I researched more about Jacob's story, I came to understand that his dream was given to him to show that God was not only present with him on his journey but also that God would fulfill His promise to Abraham, Jacob's grandfather, by making him into a great nation. This vision and accompanying confirmation from a stranger's texted prayer gave my mother peace that God was with Vaughn and that He was actively answering our prayers for complete healing.

My mother had another prophetic dream a few days later. She is a very creative yet meticulous watercolor artist. As an artist, she spends her days painting and framing for art shows, exhibits, and buyers. In her prayer journal, she wrote about a vivid dream she had involving her mentor, her art teacher for 25 years.

In the dream, my mother's mentor pointed out that one of her paintings was wrapped in linen, with an iron steaming the back of it. My mother instantly knew something was very wrong with her painting, and her mentor was covering it up with linen to fix it.

"We can fix the painting like this, and everything will be like fresh paint. We will be able to move the paint around the paper and fix it," her mentor said.

"I can't believe you knew how to do this!" My mother excitedly responded in her dream.

With watercolor, you can't cover your mistakes by adding more paint like with other, more forgiving mediums like oil and acrylic. Once a paint color is applied to watercolor paper, it's nearly impossible to change it without damaging the paper or making the colors muddy.

In the dream, her mentor unwrapped the linen and showed my mother the result. The painting was perfect! All the colors were arranged just where they needed to be for a beautiful painting. My mother wrote in her journal that her mentor knew she could win with the fixed painting. That means this painting was intended to be exhibited, and that her mentor wanted it to be a winning piece.

When my mother woke from her dream, there was a text from her mentor on her phone. She hadn't talked to her mentor about what was going on with Vaughn that week in the hospital, so getting a text that morning seemed very surprising. Did God prompt a text to remind her of the dream?

In her journal explaining the dream, she wrote, "God will fix Vaughn like new." After further reflection on her dream, I had the revelation that God was revealing much more to her in this dream than my mother initially understood.

After taking Jesus down from the cross, Joseph of Arimathea wrapped Jesus's body in fine linen cloth and laid it in a tomb (Mark 15:46). That was three days before Jesus's resurrection—His victory over death. According to the date on my mother's journal, she recorded that she had the dream on May 26, 2023, which was exactly *three days before* we received the news of Vaughn's cleared MRI, that his oxygen support was fully lowered, and in the evening, he drank his first *full* bottle of milk.

I realize now that not only was God showing my mother that Vaughn would be healed, but He was giving her the *timing* of when she would see it!

It was noteworthy that the painting was intended as an exhibit piece, and her mentor encouraged her to win once the painting was fixed. This is a direct connection to the theme of victory I held onto so tightly over Vaughn. God was declaring Vaughn's victory in my mother's dream and telling her when she would see it—just like the woman's drawing I received, also dating the very day we saw Vaughn's healing victory.

Perhaps God was also communicating in my mother's dream that Vaughn's healing is like a priceless painting meant to be shared on display.

They triumphed over him by the blood of the Lamb and
by the word of their testimony;
(Revelation 12:11, NIV, emphasis added)

In hindsight, we don't always see God's plan and answers in prayer during our battles, but this experience of looking back with fresh eyes and an open heart revealed God's answers to our prayers over Vaughn every step of the way.

DOES GOD ANSWER ALL PRAYERS?

One of the pressing questions I had about the prayers over my son was if there was some quota that God waited for us to meet for a miracle. We see the world encouraging us to approach God in prayer by gathering as many people for our cause as possible. So, what is the prayer quota for a miracle—100, 1,000, 10,000, 100,000?

Nowadays, there are social media prayer groups, prayer apps, and online community prayer threads to follow and pray for someone's healing journey. In some groups, you can see thousands of people interacting with one another on a particular prayer request.

Over the past two years, I've heard of prayer groups, communities, and even church congregations praying for Vaughn from coast to coast. Vaughn's story spread quickly, to the point that I discovered one church had mentioned his healing in their Easter Sunday Service nearly two years later in their message about the resurrection power of Jesus.

Even though I know that hundreds, perhaps even a thousand people, prayed over Vaughn's life, the answer I received to this question may be the most important one I received about prayer during this entire journey.

The Bible doesn't emphasize *how many* should pray, other than being in agreement with each other in prayer; it speaks a lot about *who* is doing the praying and *how* they pray that matters.

*Therefore confess your sins to each other and pray for each other so that **you may be healed**. The prayer of a righteous person is **powerful and effective.***
(*James 5:16, NIV, emphasis added*)

*The Lord is far from the wicked, but **he hears the
prayers of the righteous.***
(Proverbs 15:29, NIV, emphasis added)

*"Now we know that God does not hear sinners; but if
**anyone is a worshiper of God and does His will, He
hears him."***
(John 9:31, NKJV, emphasis added)

*"**Because he loves me,"** says the Lord, "I will rescue him;
I will protect him, for he acknowledges my name. He
will call on me, and I will answer him; I will be with
him in trouble, I will deliver him and honor him. With
long life I will satisfy him and show him my salvation."*
(Psalm 91:14-16, NIV, emphasis added)

*"**If you remain in me and my words remain in you,**
ask whatever you wish, and it will be done for you."*
(John 15:7, NIV, emphasis added)

*But the **salvation of the righteous** is from the Lord;
He is their strength in the time of trouble.
And **the Lord shall help them and deliver them;***
(Psalm 37:39-40, NKJV, emphasis added)

I've come to find that God isn't a giant figure in the sky with His
arms folded just waiting to hear a certain quota of prayers before
He gets up and does something about a situation. God is spirit, and

because we believe and confess in Jesus, He dwells in us through His Holy Spirit (John 4:24, 1 John 4:13), and when we abide in Him, we can be confident in prayer.

I believe it's those who pray led by His Spirit in faith who move the mountains and see victory because it is *aligned* with God's victory (Matthew 17:20-21). It is impossible to please God without faith (Hebrews 11:6).

It is the prayer from the person whose *heart* is aligned with God's Word and ready to follow His will while also praying without a shadow of a doubt that He delivers (James 1:6). The prayers from the person who loves God with all of their heart, soul, mind, and strength while living in love and forgiveness with others (Matthew 22:37, 1 John 3:22-24, Mark 11:25). When we are living in step with God's Word, and allow the Holy Spirit to direct our prayers, we not only align with God's will over the situation, but we may receive valuable insight into what we are praying over through His Spirit.

---

*And pray in the Spirit **on all occasions** with all kinds of prayers and requests.*
(Ephesians 6:18, NIV, emphasis added)

*In the same way, the **Spirit helps us** in our weakness. We do not know what we ought to pray for, but the **Spirit himself intercedes for us** through wordless groans.*
(Romans 8:26, NIV, emphasis added)

---

*...by building yourselves up in your **most holy faith***
and praying in the Holy Spirit.
(Jude 1:20, NIV, emphasis added)

When I questioned some of the prayers that were aligned, in agreement, and spoken in faith over Vaughn's healing, I found that many people who prayed allowed themselves to be led by the Holy Spirit and God's Word in their intercessory prayers for Vaughn. The Holy Spirit guides our prayers so that we speak what needs to be said. You never know what prophetic words you are praying that might lead to a miracle of healing.

*"But when he, the Spirit of truth, comes, **he will guide***
***you into all the truth**. He will not speak on his own; he*
will speak only what he hears, and he will tell you what
is yet to come."
(John 16:13, NIV, emphasis added)

The Bible also gives us a framework for effective prayer. Jesus gave us clear instructions on how to pray. He said that prayer is a very personal and intimate experience, and having an active prayer life is a personal relationship with God that is not only done in private behind closed doors but also not speaking a lot of repetitive words (Matthew 6:6-8). The strongest relationships I have are with people I feel most vulnerable with, those who understand my concerns, weaknesses, strengths, and hopes, and I theirs. Jesus was highlighting that prayer is a relationship that requires *heartfelt conversations*, not speaking repetitive words we think we are supposed to say. Because of Jesus, our relationship with God is personal and intimate.

In the Old Testament, there was an appointed High Priest who was the mediator between the people and God. The High Priest was only allowed to go into the Holy of Holies, where God's presence resided, and make atonement and intercessory prayer on behalf of others. If fact, it was so holy that if anyone went into the Most Holy Place without authorization, they would die (Leviticus 16:2-3).

Jesus came to be our Great High Priest forever, so that we can go to God's throne boldly on behalf of others and ourselves to have a personal and intimate relationship with God. God doesn't only reside in a church or cathedral, but in us through Jesus Christ (Ephesians 2:21-22, 1 Corinthians 3:16, 1 Corinthians 6:19). He lives in us through His Spirit, and anytime we pray by coming boldly to the throne of grace through Jesus, we are in the temple of God's presence.

---

*Therefore, since we have a **great high priest** who has ascended into heaven, Jesus the Son of God, let us hold firmly to the faith we profess. For we do not have a high priest who is unable to empathize with our weaknesses, but we have one who has been tempted in every way, just as we are—yet he did not sin. **Let us then approach God's throne of grace with confidence, so that we may receive mercy and find grace to help us in our time of need.***

(Hebrews 4:14-16, NIV, emphasis added)

Knowing that God answers prayers activated by faith led me to question why we don't always see the mountains move or miracles take shape right when we ask.

I don't want to position God as a magic genie who gives us everything we wish or pray for, but I want to share that God has given us very specific direction in His Word on how to stand through trials and *hold onto* our faith and trust in Him. When our circumstances change, we know we can rely on God because He is faithful and is the same yesterday, today, and tomorrow (Hebrews 13:8).

*Let us hold fast the confession of our hope **without wavering, for He who promised is faithful.***
(Hebrews 10:23, NKJV, emphasis added)

*My brethren, count it all joy when you fall into various trials, knowing that the **testing of your faith produces patience.** But let patience have its perfect work, **that you may be perfect and complete, lacking nothing**.*
(James 1:2-4, NKJV, emphasis added)

I realize that I'll never know if there were just a few prayers that were most effective in my son's miraculous healing or if it was a thousand, but I do know without any doubt that God heard every prayer from those who love Him, trust Him, and spoke faith in *His victory* for my son even before we saw it. God is faithful, and when we hold onto hope to see His goodness and plan over our situation, we may see the mountains move before our eyes (Matthew 17:20).

Chapter Five

THE BLOCKS

DRAWING CLOSER TO GOD

"One of the most significant things that happened during my search was the renewing of my mind..."

Before I was emotionally ready to analyze the prayers and speak to some who prayed fervently for Vaughn's healing, I spent months studying to understand how prayer works, what happens when we pray, and how God has directed us to pray.

After I shared parts of Vaughn's story, I was asked to pray for people in need of profound healing. This placed a burden of responsibility on me. Because my son had received a miracle, I felt somehow responsible to pray for miracles for others, especially children in need of healing. But soon this burden became too heavy, and so I dug deeper into my spiritual studies to see if God could redirect my understanding and give me answers I was so thirsty for.

I spent hours each day immersing myself in God's Word—praying, listening to sermons on prayer, watching hours of online testimonies of healing, and participating in Christian online conferences and Bible courses. I was spiritually starving for knowledge from God about prayer. There was not enough time in the day for me to be reading the Bible or listening to sermons. Many incredible spiritual experiences occurred while I drew closer to God during this time. One of the most significant things that happened during my search was the renewing of my mind (Romans 12:2), in the way I viewed myself, the way I viewed God, the way I responded to situations, and the wisdom I received for all of the answers I so craved.

After hearing many teachings about spiritual barriers in our relationship with God, I was reminded of my own one afternoon while I was getting ready to head to the grocery store. When I put on my shoe, I felt something hard inside. Vaughn must have slipped something into my shoe while he was playing. I laughed it off as I removed a yellow ball from my shoe—an easy problem to solve. As I put on my right shoe, I felt something else inside. Not just one, but many tiny blocks were inside my shoe. What I thought was an easy fix turned out to be a metaphorical clown car of blocks. I felt like God wanted me to also remove the blocks in my relationship with Him.

I was so thirsty for God during those months because God was revealing all the blocks in my heart and mind that kept me from growing closer to Him. They were indeed spiritual barriers to experiencing the fullness of His power and purpose in my life, and perhaps even blocking me from the answers I was searching so deeply for around my son's miraculous healing. As much as I wanted to get my boots on and walk out the door, God was showing me that I had some work to do to remove those blocks before my feet could comfortably fit into the shoes He had prepared for me to wear.

REMOVING BLOCKS OF FEAR

The Bible makes it very clear that we are in a battle against things that go beyond just our natural senses.

For our struggle is not against flesh and blood, but against the rulers, against the authorities, against the powers of this dark world and against the spiritual forces of evil in the heavenly realms.
(Ephesians 6:14, NIV)

Be sober, be vigilant, because your adversary the devil

> *walks about like a roaring lion,*
> ***seeking whom he may devour.***
> *(1 Peter 5:8, NKJV, emphasis added)*

It stood out to me that 1 Peter 5:8 doesn't say that the devil will devour me; it says whom he *may* devour. This is a significant distinction I see preserved in the King James Version. In the original Greek, the verb translated as "devour" is *katapiein*, which means "to devour or to swallow up," and, since it follows the word "seeking," it conveys intent or potential for harm rather than a certainty.[15] This means that I was *allowing* the fear to consume my mind in some capacity.

In Chapter One, I shared that I suffered from intense anxiety and post-traumatic stress after Vaughn was born. After we battled for Vaughn's life, I went straight into another battle: fear. I let my mind run wild with anxious thoughts daily, and it caused strife in my home. There were moments when Chris and I were yelling at each other because of things that caused me intense anxiety, or my actions made him and others feel unwelcome because of my need to control situations to keep my mind and son safe. If I cleaned things, kept my son protected, and mitigated as much risk as possible, this fear would go away. But it only *fed* it.

Without knowing it at the time, I was welcoming the roaring lion right into my home through the *deceptive* door of fear.

Just before Vaughn turned two years old, my fear turned into torment. I was having intense dreams at night that were terrifying—

fighting monsters and seeing a lot of death. I was fearful during the day and afraid in my dreams at night.

I suspect God knows fear is one of the biggest battles we face, because in my own study using a concordance, I found that the Bible mentions "fear" almost as often as it mentions "love"—at least in the King James Version. This emphasis on fear is surprising, given how central love is to our understanding of God. As 1 John 4:8 reminds us, "Whoever does not love does not know God, because God is love."

It wasn't until I started diving into God's Word daily that I was able to strengthen and renew my mind to fight this unwelcome but real battle.

*Therefore **submit** to God. **Resist** the devil and he will flee from you.*
(James 4:7, NKJV, emphasis added)

After reading James 4:7 repeatedly, I realized there were two calls to action. First, I needed to *submit* myself to God, and second, I needed to *resist*.

The word "submit" in its original Greek is *hypotagēte*, which is a verb of the Greek word *hupotassō*. This was a military term in ancient Greek that meant to be in formation and under the command of a leader.[16] It means to take a position under a higher authority. This was a clear direction from God that my attempts to control things around me would not get rid of the fear tormenting my mind. I needed to get in line, in formation, under the safety and leadership of God, because I was clearly under attack by fear.

The word "resist" in its original Greek is *antistēte*, which is a verb of the Greek word *anthistēmi*. This means so much more in its original form than it does in English:[17]

"To stand against"   *"Contrary position"*   *"To resist"*

"To oppose"   *"To set against"*   *"Ardently withstand"*

Our simpler English doesn't serve those seeking a deeper understanding, like myself. "Resist" might give the impression upon first read that it could be a passive command, as if to say avoid doing wrong things, and that is what it takes to overcome. But in reality, it's a very *active* call to action. I now view this as a step forward, not a retreating step back. If I were to express this in its simplest form, the call to action to resist could be our "no!"

It was noon on a Sunday, a dreaded time for some parents with feisty toddlers who resist the three-letter word "nap." Vaughn looked at me with as much gumption and determination as any two-year-old can have and said, "No! No nap!"

This went on for a few minutes as I pushed back at my two-year-old with another firm, "Yes, nap! Yes, nap now!"

This battle next involved a bit of chasing as my son decided to make a run for it from his room to our room. He found a cozy place to hide inside Chris's closet. I started to strategize a battle plan in my mind. But, ultimately, I gave up the chase and realized it was not worth the fight and time it would take to coerce my little ninja into an afternoon rest.

In that moment, my son showed me just how resisting a "no" can be! I wasn't practicing Biblical control of my mind, and instead of letting anxious thoughts run out of my mind like my son running out of the room, I let those thoughts run all over me. Even my toddler can stand his ground when he exercises and understands the effectiveness of his emphatic "no!"

There are many sermons and testimonies I've heard that speak to the power of using our "no," and hearing those sparked a confirmation in my spirit, leading me to remember when this simple word was a part of my miracle story as well.

It was the moment they told me my son was dead.

My immediate reaction was to take a stand against that roaring lion trying to devour me face-to-face. "No," I don't accept that my son is dead, and "God, why?" As if I was trying to say, "God, I know you are greater than this; how can the lion be in my camp taking my child?"

My mother, in that same moment, also resisted the enemy with her "no," when she cried out, "No, Jesus, No!"

*Therefore God also has highly exalted Him and given Him **the name which is above every name,** that **at the name of Jesus** every knee should bow, of those in heaven, and of those on earth, and of those under the earth, and that every tongue should confess that Jesus Christ is Lord, to the glory of God the Father.*
(Philippians 2:9-11, NKJV, emphasis added)

The devil may be the lion of fear, but Jesus is the Lion of Victory (Revelation 5:5). A counterfeit king uses fear to rule, but Jesus is the one true King, who became the Lamb of sacrifice so that we might have God's ultimate protection and power over our circumstances.

I believe God reminded me of this moment to show me how miraculous things can turn around when I *submit* the situation under His name and resist. It is also important to note that, prior to my mother and me both saying "no," my family had already been praying for God's intervention over Vaughn. I believe my family's prayers were also a powerful form of resistance.

Renewing my mind to overcome fear was not overnight. It was a battle that lasted months. I took every anxious thought, emotion, and urge to react negatively or accusatorily and consciously stopped them. I *resisted* the impulses of fear and counteracted lies with God's truth.

*... bringing **every thought into captivity** to the*
obedience of Christ,
(2 Corinthians 10:5, NKJV, emphasis added)

*There is **no fear in love**; but perfect love casts out fear,*
***because fear involves torment**. But he who fears has*
not been made perfect in love.
(1 John 4:18, NKJV, emphasis added)

I cannot tell you how much love and joy started to flow in our home when I took more responsibility over my thoughts and began to resist the fear and anxiety. I focused on God's Word day and night,

Bible verses covered my mirrors, my computer and office walls, the fridge, and even my son's changing table. If a thought came in that didn't align with God's Word, then I blocked it from taking root.

---

*Finally, brothers and sisters, whatever is **true**, whatever is **noble**, whatever is **right**, whatever is **pure**, whatever is **lovely**, whatever is **admirable**—if anything is **excellent** or **praiseworthy**—think about such things.*
(Philippians 4:8, NIV, emphasis added)

*For God has **not given us a spirit of fear**, but of power and of love and of a sound mind.*
(2 Timothy 1:7, NKJV, emphasis added)

It didn't take long for those tormenting dreams to turn into peaceful nights of rest. My mornings changed from stressing and rushing to dedicating that time to prayer and reading God's Word.

When you lie down, you will not be afraid, when you lie down, your sleep will be sweet.
(Proverbs 3:24, NIV)

One morning while praying, I had a waking vision. A lion was roaring in my face. But when I outstretched my hand over its mane, it calmly lay down to my side. I fearlessly walked past the counterfeit lion of fear and saw my path out of darkness without looking back. It was in that moment that I knew I had finally conquered the fear that had rooted so deeply in me, and I saw it tamed with my renewed mind.

REMOVING BLOCKS OF LIES

The more I searched for answers and drew closer to God's Word, my perspective of God began to shift. He opened my eyes to the lies I held onto that drove some of the questions about Vaughn's miraculous healing.

God is not the author of confusion but of peace (1 Corinthians 14:33). My confusion was only going to be resolved by my drawing closer to the author of peace, knowledge, and all wisdom.

____

But God has revealed them to us through His Spirit. For the Spirit searches all things, yes, the deep things of God.
(1 Corinthians 2:10, NKJV)

"Ask, and it will be given to you; seek, and you will find; knock, and it will be opened to you."
(Matthew 7:7, NKJV)

I began this quest with the outlook and determination that I was going to get the revelations that I needed, and God delivered.

Before Vaughn turned two, I took him to an old-fashioned puppet show. This show featured a curious cat that wanted to grow a garden. I thought to myself, "Vaughn is going to love this." But I couldn't have been more wrong. As soon as they walked the little cat puppet out onto the stage, Vaughn started screaming and running for the back door. I caught him, but not before everyone's eyes were off the puppet and on us! I bribed Vaughn to stay with some snacks as we tried to lie low in the very back seats of the auditorium.

Vaughn was very skeptical of this puppet the entire show. If the puppeteer moved the string in her hand one way, the cat's paw would follow; if she pulled the string up, the cat's head would go up, and she even spoke as if the cat were really talking. Something about this did not settle well with Vaughn.

Just like Vaughn was suspicious of the puppeteer's actions and motives for moving the cat, God showed me that there was some part of this concept that I held onto in my view of Him. Although I didn't realize it at the time, I didn't understand what a close relationship with God felt like, and my understanding was limited.

My faith was stagnant; I wasn't growing in my faith until I *chose to go deeper* and draw closer to God. Once I read the Bible daily and dedicated ample time to listening and praying, I began to pay close attention to God's voice and to see the truth about who He is. God rewards those who seek Him (Hebrews 11:6).

"My sheep listen to my voice; I know them, and they
follow me."
(John 10:27, NKJV)

What led me to find out I had a wrong perspective of God and our relationship was in my search for an answer to my own condemning questions: "Was I being punished?" "Did God have to save Vaughn because I was not good enough, or worse, was it *my* fault?"

I suspect these are similar to the questions so many have when they say, "If God exists, then why do children suffer and people die from natural disasters?"

God revealed to me some critically essential revelations that helped me remove a wrong perspective of Him and gave Him access to heal me from the hidden guilt I was holding onto after the trauma.

The first revelation came when I was reading John 9, when Jesus healed the man who was born blind. The disciples of Jesus asked who sinned, this man or his parents, that he would be blind. Jesus gave an answer that surprised everyone.

---

*"Neither this man nor his parents sinned," said Jesus, "but this happened so that **the works of God might be displayed** in him."*
(John 9:3, NIV, emphasis added)

At first read, I was confused by this statement. Why would God make this man blind so that He could heal him? After more contemplation and prayer, I found this to be one of the most beautiful statements I could have read in my search for answers. The answer freed me from the guilt and shame I felt over my son's suffering, and I finally understood the *freedom in God's love, mercy, and goodness.*

This man wasn't blind, and my baby wasn't stillborn because of punishment, but rather, this man could see, and my baby boy lives because of Jesus! Instead of focusing on *how* something became broken,

God wants us to focus on *how* He can redeem.

Sometimes bad things in this world happen because it's a messed-up, broken, fallen world, far from God. And even though we are told that sin does cause a reap-and-sow effect (Galatians 6:7), we should be quicker to view outcomes through the lens of His redemptive power and grace rather than through the muddy lens of condemnation.

Wherever there is any darkness, brokenness, or trauma, there is an opportunity for God's light and presence to heal.

This is the ultimate perspective shift and I believe it is the mindset of miracles.

I found it notable that Jesus put mud on the man's eyes, and after washing them clean, the man could see. How many times have I let the lies of my perception of who God is muck up my vision to see the truth?

Instead, I focused more on my own guilt, anxiety, and fear than on trusting in God's grace, healing, and protection. And when I allowed God to wash my vision of Him, I saw the truth—my own fear may have put me in darkness, but God's grace covered it with His marvelous light (1 Peter 2:9).

"The thief comes only to steal and kill and destroy;
I have come that they may have life, and have it to
the full."
(John 10:10, NIV, emphasis added)

After I began to remove the lies and focus on truth, I came to the second revelation: the *privilege of God's promises.*

---

*For no matter how many promises God has made, **they are "Yes" in Christ**. And so through him the "Amen" is spoken by us to the glory of God.*
(2 Corinthians 1:20, NIV, emphasis added)

Jesus made God's beautiful promises available to me. The perspective of the punishing puppeteer started to melt away, and what rose in its place was the truth: I have a Heavenly Father so real and so personal that nothing could separate me from His love, protection, guidance, and peace made available to me through Jesus.

Here is my list of promises and verses that shifted my perspective on my relationship with God:

1 God's love for me is forever and unchanging
(Romans 8:38-39, Jeremiah 31:3, Isaiah 54:10)

2 God is my healer
(Isaiah 53:5, 1 Peter 2:24, Mark 16:18, Psalm 103:3, Psalm 107:20, Jeremiah 30:17, Luke 9:2)

3 God renews me
(2 Corinthians 4:16, Isaiah 40:31, Romans 12:2, Ephesians 4:23)

4 God protects me and my family
(Isaiah 54:17, Psalm 91:10, Psalm 32:7, Psalm 121:7-8, Psalm 46:1, 2 Thessalonians 3:3)

5 God gives me authority over darkness

(Romans 8:37, 1 John 5:4, Luke 10:19, 1 John 4:4, 1 Corinthians 15:57)

6 God gives me wisdom and teaches me things I need to know

(John 14:26, 1 John 2:27)

7 God hears my cry and helps me

(Mark 11:24, 1 John 5:14-15, Proverbs 15:29, Jeremiah 33:3, Psalm 18:6, Psalm 34:17, 1 Peter 3:12)

8 God gives me gifts, and I lack nothing

(Matthew 7:11, Luke 11:13, 1 Peter 4:10, Romans 12:6, 1 Corinthians 1:7)

9 God blesses me, crowns me with honor, mercies, and favor

(Psalm 8:5, Isaiah 62:3, 2 Timothy 4:8, Psalm 84:11, Psalm 103:1-5, 1 Peter 5:4, Psalm 5:12)

10 God strengthens me

(Isaiah 41:10, Philippians 4:13, Psalm 118:14, Ephesians 3:16)

11 God equips me

(Ephesians 6:13, Hebrews 13:21, 2 Timothy 3:17)

12 God gives me plans and vision for my life

(Jeremiah 29:11, Ephesians 2:10, Habakkuk 2:3, Hebrews 12:1)

13 God prospers my work

(Psalm 90:17, Deuteronomy 15:10, Ecclesiastes 3:13, Proverbs 13:11, Proverbs 10:4, Joshua 1:8)

14 God leads me to the truth

(Psalm 25:5, Psalm 119:160, John 16:13, John 14:6, John 8:32, John 4:24)

15 God gives me rest

(Matthew 11:28-30, Exodus 33:14, Hebrews 4:9-10, Psalm 62:5, Psalm 23:2)

16 God gives me peace

(John 14:27, Philippians 4:7, Isaiah 26:3, Romans 15:13, Psalm 29:11, Isaiah 9:6, 2 Thessalonians 3:16)

17 God gives me grace through Christ, forgives me, and I am free from shame

(Colossians 3:13, Matthew 6:12, Isaiah 43:25, Ephesians 1:7-8, Romans 8:1, 1 John 1:9, Hebrews 10:22, Hebrews 8:12, Psalm 103:12)

18 God gives me life

(Psalm 118:17, John 6:63, John 11:25-26, Romans 8:11)

19 God never leaves me

(Hebrews 13:5, Deuteronomy 31:6)

20 God calls me His adopted child, co-heir in Christ, and His chosen

(Romans 8:14-17, 1 Peter 2:9)

REMOVING BLOCKS OF UNFORGIVENESS

Because I love pleasantly scented lotions, hair, and beauty products, our master bathroom quickly turned into my husband's nightmare. What started as a modest collection soon took over every surface and shelf in our bathroom. I purchased a vanity with a built-in mirror and sliding drawers to organize my accumulated products. What was initially my gift became Chris's gift when he was now spared from having to see the clutter.

My favorite feature of this modern farmhouse vanity was the light around the mirror with three different modes of brightness. It wasn't long before Vaughn discovered the buttons on mommy's vanity and made it his mission to climb the chair to reach the magic lighted mirror!

As I drew closer to God by reading the Bible daily, I found that it was like looking in the mirror of my new vanity. It reflected things about myself in different modes of brightness that I needed to *change, repair,* or *illuminate.*

---

*But we all, with unveiled face, beholding **as in a mirror** the glory of the Lord, **are being transformed into the same image from glory to glory,** just as by the Spirit of the Lord.*
(2 Corinthians 3:18, NKJV, emphasis added)

It not only shed light and direction on the fear and anxiety in my mind, but also on the destruction of my relationship at my own hands. It reflected back to me the pain I caused by breaking trust in my marriage.

Every time I told my husband he did something wrong, every time

I showed anxiety after he made a decision, and every time I yelled or lost control because I was impulsively fearful about something, I was destroying the trust in our relationship.

The wise woman builds her house,
But the foolish pulls it down with her hands.
(Proverbs 14:1, NKJV)

God showed me the way to complete healing, not only in the renewing of my mind but also in the renewing of every relationship in my life, pushing back the darkness. The Bible became the brightest mirror in my life, which also became my biggest beauty regimen. The more I strived to become like Jesus and think how God wanted me to think, the more beautiful I felt and seemed to others, including my husband.

After praying one evening and feeling led by the Holy Spirit, I grabbed Chris's hand, asked for his forgiveness, and listed all the things that came to mind that may have caused harm to our relationship by my hands through fear.

"You don't know how much this means to me," Chris replied. "I didn't know how much I needed to hear you say these things until I heard them."

This entire time, I didn't know the extent of the destruction my fear was causing in our relationship, but I trusted God's leading to initiate the repair. God's mirror never reflects what is not true. He leads us into *all* truth, and He knew what was troubling Chris's heart even though I didn't (Matthew 5:23-24). Forgiveness sets us free!

God's Word also reflected back at me how God sees me. This empowered my self-esteem more than any new mascara or haircut could ever do, and it gave me confidence. When I looked at myself, I no longer saw my physical flaws, the pushing 40-year-old wrinkles, sun damage spots, or smile lines, but I saw someone who was loved beyond all measure (Ephesians 3:19), someone who was gifted and part of a chosen family in Christ.

It wasn't until I went through the time of drawing close to God that my mind was renewed, and joy in my heart *overfilled me* to *overcome* the trauma.

After this, I was finally ready to read and analyze the prayers over Vaughn, and to my surprise, I found one that was just for me. This prayer was written by a woman I've never met and who didn't know me, but it was answered two years later.

"Lord, we have so many questions that seem impossible to answer. But we pray, Jesus that you in your mercy and grace would give Kelly exactly what her heart needs to have peace. Father, anoint her head with oil. Your oil of Joy! That she will no longer remember the pain, but we remove from her that garment of heaviness and place on her your garment of praise. Jesus, we declare she has your mind! She listens to your voice and another she will not hear. We ask for intimate moments for just the two of you to go away and be refreshed. She is so precious and tenderly loved by you! Wrap her up in the cocoon of your arms, and may it be so apparent that the darts of the enemy do not prosper. AMEN!"

In this journey of processing, healing, and removing the blocks and barriers in my relationship with God, I saw God's steadfast love through it all, and I was finally ready to put on the shoes of *peace* that God had prepared for me to wear from the very beginning (Ephesians 6:15).

You will keep him in perfect peace,
Whose mind is stayed on You,
Because he trusts in You.
(Isaiah 26:3, NKJV, emphasis added)

Chapter Six

THE FAITH
THREADS OF VICTORY

"*Something happens* in us when we contend and pray for the healing of others; it gives us a front-row seat to the power of prayer, which strengthens our faith for our own time of need."

"This one?" I directed Vaughn's attention to a small horse with a bright red saddle.

"No..." Vaughn sighed.

"Ok, what about this one?!" I patted the seat of a large, shiny gorilla with a menacing face, trying to make it more appealing.

"No, Mommy, this one!" Vaughn's eyes lit up as he pointed to the largest white horse with a brilliant blue saddled seat.

"That's perfect, great choice!" I scooped up his tiny toddler body, placing him on one of the tallest rides on the carousel.

"Hold on!" I directed his hands to the gold pole in front of him as I wrapped the black seatbelt around his waist and buckled it tightly.

The giant horse began to move steadily up and down.

Vaughn looked at me nervously, as if he were already regretting his decision to choose a high seat on the ride. I smiled, reassuring him that it would be safe and fun. His anxiety turned into pure excitement once the music started playing. To my surprise, it was Phil Collins singing "You'll Be In My Heart." This was a song I frequently sang to Vaughn to help him fall asleep at night when he was a baby.

As our perspective shifted with the rotation of the carousel, my husband Chris came into view, waving at us as we passed by. Chris thought it would be amusing to run alongside the carousel to keep himself in our sight. Vaughn giggled, imagining that he was chasing his daddy on a large horse.

I watched, smiling, and reflected on how many turns it took over the last two years to change my perspective on the *power* of faith.

Faith is going for the big horse, even though you can't get up there by yourself. It's reaching for something so great you can only get there with God by your side.

I can do all things through Christ who strengthens me.
(Philippians 4:13, NKJV)

In October 2023, a few months after Vaughn was home from the hospital, one of my close friends, who was in the intimate text thread of my requested prayer warriors, was diagnosed with an aggressive stage IV inflammatory breast cancer that had metastasized to her hip and rib bones over a matter of weeks. The initial doctors told her that they had no intent to cure with surgery and to send her to palliative care.

After the shock, she used her innermost "no" to resist the roaring lion of fear. Because she witnessed the miracle of Vaughn's victory, she was empowered to believe for her own healing. She changed her mindset from fear to *faith* and built up her trust and relationship with God to conquer cancer. She found a doctor who treated her aggressively with chemo, and she attended a prayer conference where she received prayer to stand against the fear and overcome.

In just five months of treatment and successful surgery, she miraculously defeated the aggressive cancer. She was named at a Pink Tie Charity Ball a year later, and in her bio featured on the large screen behind her were the words, "helping women be *victorious* over cancer."

God's thread of victory in our story may have started with the prayers over my son, but they didn't end there—they continued like ripples breaking barriers of faith.

When my friend initially saw the overwhelming and difficult treatment choices in front of her, just like my son, she went for the biggest ride possible—Jesus on the white horse.

I saw heaven standing open and there before me was a **white horse, whose rider is called Faithful and True.**

On his robe and on his thigh he has this name written: *KING OF KINGS AND LORD OF LORDS.*
(Revelation 19:11, 16, NIV, emphasis added)

When we hold tightly to the victory of Jesus over our circumstances, faith begins to take root, and fear begins to melt away. Something happens in us when we contend and pray for the healing of others; it gives us a front-row seat to the power of prayer, which strengthens our faith for our own time of need (James 5:16).

Later, my friend hosted a birthday party to celebrate her victory over cancer with close friends and family. After most of us had eaten and the party was dwindling, a woman walked in the front door.

I introduced myself and I found out that she lived across the street and had a newborn at home which is why she and her husband came in shifts to the party.

"This is Vaughn's mom! The baby you prayed for!" my friend said excitedly as she insisted the woman take a wrapped plate of food home with her.

The woman's expression changed. She looked at me and said my boy was a miracle and she held onto my son's story for strength while her new baby was in the NICU. She'd just arrived home after a long and trying two months in the hospital. I believe that because she prayed for my son, and she saw God's goodness in our son's healing, more than 18 months later, she had stronger faith during her own baby's recovery.

God connects our stories in prayer like a beautiful tapestry woven together. One thread connects to another, and then to another, and so on. Only God can see how all of the threads weave together for the good of those who love Him (Romans 8:28).

God knew what was going to happen to each of these women who prayed for my son, and it was no accident that their faith was strengthened before they faced their own trials. I believe God's plan for victory is also one big tapestry *knit* by our love for Jesus and others.

[For my hope is] that their hearts may be encouraged
as they are knit together in [unselfish] love, *so that*
they may have all the riches that come from the full
assurance of understanding [the joy of salvation],
resulting in a true [and more intimate] knowledge of
the mystery of God, that is, Christ.
(Colossians 2:2, AMP, emphasis added)

Perhaps this is a glimpse into how God designed the Kingdom of Heaven to operate here on Earth, that we would build each other up in faith and prayer so that we might also be built up in faith and prayer when we need it (Galatians 6:2).

Another thread in our tapestry of victory was redemption over loss. I mentioned that when I was six months pregnant, we decided to name Vaughn after Chris's father, who passed away in 2020. During that time, our family was unable to grieve normally due to the heavy COVID-19 shutdown restrictions. The day his father had the heart attack on Friday, March 13, 2020 was just two days before the entire nation shut down. I remember sitting in an empty waiting room of the hospital, watching the news of a looming pandemic.

Because of the shutdowns, my father-in-law wasn't allowed to have regular visitation, and I couldn't see him during the month he was in the hospital; only one pre-approved person for a few hours. Chris wasn't even able to be there when his father passed because of this restriction. Even after he passed, his death certificate labeled that he died from COVID-19, which could not have been further from the truth. This confusion caused tension with the funeral home and added complications to the funeral arrangement process.

I remember standing outside the cemetery, trying to catch a glimpse of the funeral through the gates, as only four people were allowed to enter beyond them. Even as a daughter-in-law, I wasn't allowed to enter and comfort my grieving husband during the funeral. Common sense went right out the window for grieving families during that time, and I can only imagine how many other families also suffered as a result of the pandemic fear.

This was a moment in our new marriage that we weren't prepared for; it took the breath out of us. Sadness was in our home for the next two years, which was not an expected start to our new life together.

When I became pregnant, however, the sadness turned to excitement, and deciding to name our baby, Vaughn, after Chris's father seemed like a way to celebrate and grieve at the same time. Knowing his father would never meet his son was like a hole that Chris could never fill, but somehow the name felt like a way for his son and father to be connected.

I can't forget the moment the doctor came out to brief us on my father-in-law's condition for the first time.

"You need to understand, he had [roughly] 40 minutes of CPR, and now he is critical," the doctor said to all of us in the waiting room.

"We're going to airlift him to a more equipped hospital. They have an ECMO machine that will be able to recirculate the oxygen in his blood."

Looking back, this was the same talk track we heard for Vaughn. Vaughn received a similar time of prolonged CPR, and he was also medevacked to a new hospital because they had the ECMO machine and a more advanced cardiac unit. But, as previously mentioned, something happened when they were preparing the machine for Vaughn upon his arrival—he started improving.

My father-in-law's heart, lungs, and body were so damaged after the CPR that he didn't survive a month of treatment at one of the world's leading cardiac hospitals. How could a newborn, who also received extended CPR, but was pronounced dead, suddenly take a breath and then make a full recovery in just two weeks? What did the suffering of my father-in-law have to do with Vaughn's healing?

Looking back at the uncanny similarities between my father-in-law's suffering and Vaughn's healing is almost too difficult to comprehend naturally. I mentioned in the previous chapter that when I committed to reading the Bible more regularly, I began to find spiritual connections and answers to all of my questions. When I re-read the story of Joseph in Genesis, I saw so many connections that opened my eyes to things I had never understood before in our own story of grief and healing (*read* Genesis 37-47).

I noticed many spiritual similarities between it and our own. When my father-in-law had his heart attack at the start of the pandemic, we felt like Jacob seeing the coat of his beloved Joseph drenched in blood. It was a shock that immediately sparked a loss of hope. I can't speak for everyone in our family at that time, but I do know that Chris and I were not praying great prayers of faith for God's victory. A wave of fear and grief crashed over us, and we got *swallowed* up in it.

And when I was pregnant, it felt like we had a renewal of hope and joy. Jacob might have felt similar with his youngest son, Benjamin, in that Benjamin was his new hope and joy after losing his beloved wife and Joseph. And if Jacob lost Benjamin, he said he would not survive the sorrow.

---

whose life is closely bound up with the boy's life,
(Genesis 44:30, NIV)

Seeing Vaughn suffer in the same way his father did was so diffi-cult for Chris. I don't know what would have happened to Chris if our son had also died in the same way, but it would have been a painful road for Chris to recover emotionally and spiritually. In other words, at that time, his spiritual life was *bound up* with his son's life.

When Jacob heard the news that Joseph was alive, the Bible says that his spirit was "revived" (Genesis 45:27). When Chris saw victo-ry after his son conquered the same suffering with his father's name, it was like Chris's spirit was also revived. He felt that his father was redeemed in a way through the victory of Vaughn's healing and saw God's goodness through it all.

*"**You intended to harm me, but God intended it for good** to accomplish what is now being done, the saving of many lives."*
(Genesis 50:20, NIV, emphasis added)

The enemy planned to drive our family further from God with deeper pain. Still, when we submitted the situation to God completely, and we trusted in His promises and goodness while praying in faith to take a stand in agreement, we saw the true plan that God had for our family – victory.

Just like God directed Joseph serving the king to prepare all of Egypt for the famine, He directs us to store and build up our faith so that when the enemy deceives us by presenting us with our beloved's robe covered in goat's blood, we're prepared to cover it in the blood of the Lamb.

No matter how dire the situation looks, we can choose to have the faith to resist giving in to the worst-case scenario and instead *trust* in God, who is our great deliverer, and pray for His plan.

*They triumphed over him by the **blood of the Lamb**...*
(Revelation 12:11, NIV, emphasis added)

*"For I know the plans I have for you," declares the LORD, "**plans to prosper you and not to harm you,** plans to give you hope and a future."*
(Jeremiah 29:11, NIV, emphasis added)

Who shall separate us from the love of Christ? Shall tribulation, or distress, or persecution, or famine, or nakedness, or peril, or sword? ...
Yet in all these things we are more than conquerors through Him who loved us.
(Romans 8:35,37, NKJV)

It is no coincidence that Chris and I felt so strongly that our boy was to be named Vaughn after my father-in-law. God knew what was going to happen to Vaughn. And this was an opportunity not only for healing from grief but also for redemption over what the enemy had stolen from our family.

No one could have crafted a better redemption but God. Our hearts are like spiritual storehouses; they can be empty during a famine or full of life-saving nourishment when we need it.

*Then Jesus declared, "I am the bread of life. **Whoever comes to me will never go hungry,** and **whoever believes in me will never be thirsty."***
(*John 6:35, NIV, emphasis added*)

I find that when I ask God for answers, He reveals spiritual truths, as He did for me with Joseph's story. Once I finished reading Joseph's story and seeing the connections to our own, I realized I had forgotten that, although not of Egyptian heritage, my father-in-law was born in Egypt, and his father served the king when my father-in-law was a boy.

We are just threads in a greater tapestry of God's victory.

Chapter Seven

THE VICTORY
BREATH IN EVERY BATTLE

"Some moments in life will leave us breathless, but it's God's breath that leads us to overcome."

I vividly remember the first time I got the wind knocked out of me. I was twelve years old, and it was the '90s when skateparks and skateboards were *all the rage*, as we would say. I took a lot of my what's cool cues from my older brother, who was very much into skating. One afternoon, we decided to go to a new skatepark near our house. My brother went to skateboard on the larger ramps, imagining he was like *Tony Hawk*, but I stuck to the smaller ramps as I tested out my new purple inline skates.

What I didn't anticipate was that the steepness of the tiny ramps curved inward, not straight down. So, just like a cartoon walking on a banana peel, my feet flew out from under me and my upper back hit the pavement directly. I didn't understand what was happening when I couldn't breathe in. Every inhale I tried to take was a struggle for a few minutes. I learned that even the smallest ramps can knock the wind out of us if we are not prepared.

Going from *death* to *breath* is something that God wants us to master in every situation in our lives. My son received miraculous physical breath, but my testimony is that I also learned how to take God's breath in every battle. Some moments in life will leave us breathless, but it's God's breath that leads us to overcome. Whether it's the need for God's healing for your physical body, God's redemptive love to heal a relationship or hurt, or His power for deliverance from fear, God's Spirit is with us and ready to guide us if we're ready to keep His breath.

GOD'S BREATH IN THE BEGINNING

From the very beginning, God gave us physical breath.

*Then the Lord God formed a man from the dust of the ground and **breathed into** his nostrils the breath of life...*
(Genesis 2:7, NIV, emphasis added)

And the Holy Spirit was also in the very beginning.

*Now the earth was formless and empty, darkness was over the surface of the deep, and the **Spirit of God was hovering over the waters.***
(Genesis 1:2, NIV, emphasis added)

It is interesting to note that in the original Hebrew, the word used for "the Spirit" in this verse is *Ruach*, which means "breath" or "wind."[18]

God was making a way for us to receive His breath before we even existed. When His Spirit hovered over the waters of the Earth, He imagined us and planned victory for us through Jesus from the very beginning of creation.

*This grace was given us in Christ Jesus **before the beginning of time...***
(2 Timothy 1:9, NIV, emphasis added)

*For he chose us in him **before the creation of the world** to be holy and blameless in his sight.*
(Ephesians 1:4, NIV, emphasis added)

Your eyes saw my unformed body; all the days ordained
*for me were written in your book **before one of them***
came to be.
(*Psalm 139:16, NIV, emphasis added*)

This not only means that God knew me before the world was created, but He knew every battle I was about to face. How many battles have I tried to win on my own and lost because I didn't seek His wisdom and peace over which path and direction to take?

After Jesus's last breath on the cross, God made a way for all of us to receive His spiritual breath. When Jesus conquered death and revealed Himself to His disciples before His ascension, He gave them His breath—the Holy Spirit.

---

*And with that **he breathed on them** and said, "Receive*
the Holy Spirit."
(*John 20:22, NIV, emphasis added*)

Jesus also described the Holy Spirit as an audible wind.

"The wind blows wherever it pleases. You hear its sound,
but you cannot tell where it comes from or where it is
*going. **So it is with everyone born of the Spirit."***
(*John 3:8, NIV, emphasis added*)

When Jesus's followers experienced the power of the Holy Spirit for the first time, it was described as a roaring and mighty wind that filled the upper room where they were waiting (Acts 2:2).

God's Spirit is not only powerful, but given to us for wisdom, comfort, knowledge, and guidance in all situations (John 14:26).

The Holy Spirit is a gift to us when we believe and confess in Jesus (Acts 2:38, Luke 11:13, Acts 1:8). He lives in us and seals us as an adopted child of God, and we are no longer subject to the law of sin and death, but rather we can set our mind on the things of the Spirit, life and peace (Romans 8:6).

Being born of the Spirit means you are a new creation in Christ (2 Corinthians 5:17). My journey of healing began when I finally understood what it means to be a new creation and live *with* His Spirit. It means having a renewed mind to focus on true things; it means being a victor, not a victim; it means being sealed as God's chosen, loved, and favored, with no room in my heart for fear. God's Spirit in us is one of love, power, and a sound mind (2 Timothy 1:7).

Everyone who believes that Jesus is the Christ is born of
God, and everyone who loves the father loves his
child as well... And his commands are not burdensome,
for everyone born of God overcomes the world. This
is the victory that has overcome the world, *even our*
faith. Who is it that overcomes the world? ***Only the one***
who believes that Jesus is the Son of God.
(1 John 5:1-5, NIV, emphasis added)

DON'T LIMIT GOD'S POWER IN YOUR LIFE

When we understand the significance of who we are in Him, and we partner with the Holy Spirit, who directs us to walk in God's plan for our lives, we become more than conquerors. The Bible warns us not to "grieve" or "quench" the Holy Spirit (Ephesians 4:30; 1 Thessalonians 5:19). In its original Greek, "quench" is the word *sbennymi*, which means not only "to extinguish" or "to put out" but also to *suppress or stifle* the Holy Spirit.[19]

I never knew this until I went through the process of removing any blocks that stifled the Holy Spirit in my life. I was acting in my own power, which made me susceptible to fear. Instead, I needed to be strengthened by God's power, which would help me not only to stand against fear but also to *overcome* it.

---

*For the Spirit God gave us **does not make us timid**, but gives us power, love and self-discipline.*

(2 Timothy 1:7, NIV, emphasis added)

*I pray that out of his glorious riches he may strengthen you **with power** through his Spirit in your inner being...*
(Ephesians 3:16, NIV, emphasis added)

*My message and my preaching were not with wise and persuasive words, but with a **demonstration of the Spirit's power.***
(1 Corinthians 2:4, NIV, emphasis added)

Although we may be adopted sons and daughters of God through the belief and confession in Jesus Christ and have received the Holy Spirit, we not only can limit but also extinguish His power in our lives through our hearts and actions. To be clear, He never leaves us (Matthew 28:20), but He wants us to have and live in a relationship *with* Him. And this means that the Holy Spirit never pushes us to follow, but leads us in all truth and helps us in our time of need when we are receptive to Him (John 14:16).

*Since we live by the Spirit, let us **keep in step** with the Spirit.*
(Galatians 5:16, NIV, emphasis added)

The Holy Spirit is our gift, and we can choose to follow Him or ignore Him. In my experience, believing in God is not enough to live a life full of God's plans to guide and prosper us (Jeremiah 29:11). We need to be *partnered* with His Spirit and receive His breath every day, which He intended for us to have from the *beginning* of time.

***But the natural man does not receive the things of the Spirit of God**, for they are foolishness to him; nor can he know them, because they are spiritually discerned.*
(1 Corinthians 2:14, NKJV, emphasis added)

When we are full of God's breath and don't quench it, we are prepared for any unexpected situation coming our way. This is the battle plan I've learned in my journey for keeping His B-R-E-A-T-H.

B

BUILD UP YOUR FAITH IN JESUS'S VICTORY

In Isaiah's prophetic words about Jesus's life and ministry, it was prophesied that Jesus's wounds would heal us, and the same verse was later confirmed by the Apostle Peter (1 Peter 2:24) after the ministry, death, resurrection, and ascension of Jesus Christ.

*...and by his wounds we are **healed**.*
(Isaiah 53:5, NIV, emphasis added)

The root of the Hebrew word used in the original text for "healed" in Isaiah is *rapha*, which is used throughout Scripture to speak to both physical healing of the body and figurative restoration from distress, as well as to make whole.[20]

In this context, we can understand that through what Jesus endured at the cross, the atonement has been made for us to be whole with God. And because we are sealed with His Holy Spirit, we may approach God in faith to receive His healing power in our lives. When we build our faith on what Jesus has already done for us, and rely on His Spirit to direct us, we are more than conquerors. Ephesians 6 talks about the armor of God. Faith is described as our shield, which is so powerful that it can protect us and "extinguish all the flaming arrows of the evil one." Take note that it says *all* the arrows, not just some, but *all of them*!

Living *in faith* in Jesus means you have direct permission to come to the throne boldly with your needs and the needs of others; power and partnership with Him through His Spirit; and being seated with Him in heavenly places as an adopted child of God (Ephesians 2:6). When we realize the greatness of what we have in Him, our faith can help us withstand any trial.

One other revelation I received as I began to build my faith is we have the very miracle power that raised Jesus from the dead living in us—the Holy Spirit.

*Now to him who is able to do immeasurably more than all we ask or imagine, **according to his power that is at work within us.***
(Ephesians 3:20, NIV, emphasis added)

*If the **Spirit of him who raised Jesus from the dead dwells in you**, he who raised Christ Jesus from the dead will also give life to your mortal bodies through his Spirit **who dwells in you.***
(Romans 8:11, NKJV, emphasis added)

Perhaps the greatest thing I have learned and can share is that my story is not special. What I mean by this is that we didn't receive a miracle because of who we are, but we experienced God's power because of who *He is.*

*"Most assuredly, I say to you, **he who believes in Me,***

*the works that I do he will do also; and greater works than these he will do, because I go to My Father. **And whatever you ask in My name, that I will do**, that the Father may be glorified in the Son. If you ask anything in My name, I will do it."*
(John 14:12-14, NIV, emphasis added)

If you want to learn to keep God's breath in your battle, start by looking at the power in the name of Jesus.

B–R
REMOVE THE BLOCKS IN YOUR RELATIONSHIP WITH GOD

Blocks in our faith are anything in our minds or actions that take us out of alignment with God. I believe that blocks can be our unbelief, unforgiveness, disobedience, ignoring the Holy Spirit, fear, or sin. When we are out of alignment with God's will and path for us, we can spiritually *block* His power, direction, and comfort available through His Spirit.

When we shift our perspective from us to God and His Word, things start to change in our lives. The way we view situations, the way we respond, and most importantly, the relationship we have with God is strengthened.

It can be difficult for us to grasp that God never changes (Malachi 3:6). We are constantly striving, always learning, and our position and circumstances in life change. Still, God is the same yesterday, today, and tomorrow. Because God never changes, it is we who must change in our relationship with Him by renewing our minds (Romans 12:2). It is through the renewing of our minds that we can come to understand who God is and how to listen to His will and voice.

---

*Do not be deceived, **every good and perfect gift** is from above coming down from the Father of lights, **who does not change** like shifting shadows.*
(James 1:17, NIV, emphasis added)

What deceptions have you listened to about God that shifted your perspective in the wrong direction? Spend time asking God to reveal the truth and to correct your path. Once we understand who God is, we can hear His voice and discern it more clearly.

I often take Vaughn to our neighborhood park. There, they have both toddler and older kid play areas. Even before Vaughn was two, he would go to the older kid structures, seeing the higher stairs and slides as a fun adventure. Vaughn would run along the wobbly bridge, climb up the advanced ladder, and try to do what the big kids did—but with me holding his hand.

"Wow, he's brave and fast!" one mother said as she watched my little guy navigate everything without hesitation.

I immediately thought that this is how we're meant to live when we're in step with God. When we take His hand, we can go on the big adventure, and we can bravely go through all of the obstacles in front of us because we have someone stronger holding us up.

I noticed a big difference in Vaughn's behavior if he ever let go of my hand—he would be slower, more cautious, and I could see a sense of fear and hesitation rise in him. When we hold tightly to God's hand, we have a deeper connection to His strength and power. As I dove deeper into God's Word, I saw that God's hand is very prevalent throughout Scripture.

*"I will strengthen you, yes, I will help you, I will uphold you **with My righteous right hand.**
For I, the LORD your God, **will hold your right hand,**
saying to you, Fear not, I will help you."*
(Isaiah 41:10,13, NKJV, emphasis added)

*though he may stumble, he will not fall,
for the **Lord upholds him with his hand.***
(Psalm 37:24, NIV, emphasis added)

Because God never changes, we know He is always there, ready to hold our hand, but we must choose whether we will keep and follow His. We are the ones putting up the barriers in our relationship with God, not the other way around. God never changes.

Once we understand that we are in control of the things in our lives that hinder us from having a close grip with God, we can work with His Spirit and remove them (James 4:7-10). This is what it means to abide in Him.

---

*"I am the vine, you are the branches. He who abides in Me, and I in him, bears much fruit; **for without Me you can do nothing.** If anyone does not abide in Me, he is cast out as a branch and is withered; and they gather them and throw them into the fire, and they are burned. **If you abide in Me, and My words abide in you, you will ask what you desire, and it shall be done for you...**"*

(John 15:5-8, NIV, emphasis added)

God gave us His Word so that we may know His will and recognize His voice, and we have the comforting and guiding power of the Holy Spirit, who is our Helper no matter the situation (John 14:26).

The best news is that even if we make mistakes, we can come boldly to the throne of grace through Jesus Christ. There, and with His help, we can remove everything that blocks our faith and connection to His divine power and purpose for us (Hebrews 4:16). When we remove the blocks and have a firm grip on God's hand, we can stare any roaring lion in the face and have hope for God's powerful *deliverance*.

---

*I sought the Lord, and he answered me; **he delivered me from all my fears.***

(Psalm 34:4, NIV, emphasis added)

B–R–E
EMBRACE EVERY CIRCUMSTANCE WITH PRAISE

When I was in junior high school, my history class did an unconventional field trip. We did a history hike, all dressed in some Civil War clothing, and walked miles as the army would have. Because I played the flute in band, I was one of the flute players leading the charge of the class army. After a while, I remember not wanting to play the flute anymore. My feet hurt, and I probably thought it was a bit silly that a flute player would be walking ahead of everyone in battle. It became an even longer hike with a poor attitude. What I didn't know was that musicians were very important in the Civil War; they performed many duties that were critical. They set the pace for long-distance marches, gave audible cues on direction and commands in battle, and even boosted the morale of weary soldiers.[21] Had I known the true purpose of leading the battle with music, it might have kept me going longer with a better attitude.

Similarly, if we don't know why God wants us to praise Him in our battles, it may seem silly and very out of place. However, God shows us that praise during our pain is also for *our* benefit. Praise restores our spirit while helping us *stay focused on God* and what He is doing rather than the painful circumstance at hand.

---

give thanks in all circumstances; for this is God's will for
you in Christ Jesus.
(*1 Thessalonians 5:18, NIV*)

*All this is for **your benefit**, so that the grace that
is reaching more and more people **may cause
thanksgiving to overflow** to the glory of God.
Therefore we do not lose heart.*
(*2 Corinthians 4:15-16, NIV, emphasis added*)

When we prioritize praise in the midst of our battles, we shift our perspective to be more in tune with God's voice and direction. Just as the flute was ahead of the marching soldiers leading the charge, so too can worship deliver instructions from our Commanding Officer.

I will praise the Lord, who counsels me; *even at night
my heart instructs me.
I keep my eyes always on the Lord. With him **at my
right hand**, I will not be shaken.*
(*Psalm 16:7-8, NIV, emphasis added*)

In 2 Chronicles 20, Jehoshaphat, king of Judah, prioritized prayer and worship when his people faced war. After praying to God, requesting victory over two armies intent on destroying Judah, Jehoshaphat received a prophetic word from God through his musician, Jahaziel. He told Jehoshaphat to direct his people to face the two approaching armies, but not to engage in battle, because it was God's battle.

The next day, instead of soldiers, Jehoshaphat placed singers at the front of his army, instructing them to praise God as they advanced, singing, "Give thanks to the LORD, for his faithful love endures forever." During the songs of praise, God caused the two enemy armies to destroy themselves. This is a powerful story of how our praise, no matter how silly it may seem in times of fear, can be a great weapon at the forefront of our battle.

The Lord is my strength and my shield; **my heart trusts in him,** *and he helps me. My heart leaps for joy,* **and with my song I praise him.**
(Psalm 28:7, NIV, emphasis added)

When Vaughn was in the hospital, one of my aunts was fervently praying for Vaughn, and she received direction from God while she was praying. She said that I needed to sing and use my voice to praise God, and I would be renewed. I have been a singer all my life, and music was a big part of my personal creative outlet.

During that time, I used every ounce of physical and emotional strength to hold onto victory for my son that I *ignored* my own emotional pain. I told my aunt I wasn't going to sing, and it's one of the biggest regrets I have from that time. Now I know it wasn't just for God; but it was God trying to heal *me*. Had I been renewing my spirit during that time, I might have had enough faith to overcome the fear in the next battle of anxiety that came my way not too long after.

I learned praise isn't something we do when we are happy. It is something we choose to do every day in sadness or joy. It's another weapon in our armory. Now every morning in my prayer time, I praise God no matter what I'm feeling and my spirit is continually renewed.

B–R–E–A
APPOINT FAITH WARRIORS TO BATTLE WITH YOU

---

*"Truly I tell you, whatever you **bind on earth will be bound in heaven**, and whatever you **loose on earth will be loosed in heaven**. Again, truly I tell you that **if two of you on earth agree about anything they ask for, it will be done for them by my Father in heaven**. For where two or three gather in my name, there am I with them."*
(Matthew 18:18-20, NIV, emphasis added)

When we are in a serious battle, we need warriors to stand with us when we are weak in our time of trouble. But these warriors may need to be selected carefully.

I was very cautious in choosing those who would hold onto hope with me for Vaughn's miracle. I knew it was a very dire situation and an outsider could look and only see the bad news.

I firmly believe that the prayers of others strengthened our faith to hold onto God's goodness and hope in seeing His victory over our baby boy. I've seen God's wonder-working power through prayer, not only through miraculous healing, but also in guidance through difficult decisions. We will hear God's voice directing us, and He may use others listening to His voice to also confirm His plans (Matthew 18:16, 2 Corinthians 13:1).

I love the story of the paralytic man in Mark 2:1-12. Jesus was teaching in a residence in Capernaum, and the crowds piled in and outside the doorway, and no one could get through. Four friends lowered the paralytic down to Jesus by cutting a hole in the roof so he could be healed.

It would have been easy for the paralytic's friends to see the crowd and say something like, "Look, it's too difficult for your miracle today. But maybe we'll have an opportunity tomorrow." Instead, these friends climbed to the roof with the paralytic, cut a hole in the roof, and lowered him down inside. Those are the kinds of friends we need when we're looking for a miracle. We need friends who go to the throne boldly in prayer on our behalf and get our needs directly to the King of kings and the Lord of lords. We all need those crazy friends of faith.

I know that I cannot pray for everyone in the world who needs this level of prayer. But just like the story of the paralytic, there are times when a friend will come and say, "I need you to take my need to Jesus today, no matter what."

I woke up one morning to a text from an acquaintance requesting emergency prayer. I didn't want to text back, prying for all the details. As someone who's been in that situation before, I know how exhausting it can be to update people during the actual emergency. Instead, I dropped to my knees and asked the Holy Spirit to guide me because I didn't know anything about the situation and I didn't know what to pray. As soon as I asked, I had an impression of what was wrong. It was very specific and very serious. I prayed with the word of knowledge I received that morning through the Holy Spirit. Later, when I was updated, I found that the impression I had received in prayer was the exact details of that person's emergency. The Holy Spirit can supernaturally reveal things to us when we need to know them to pray in accordance with God's will (1 Corinthians 12:8).

———————

*Now He who searches the hearts knows what the mind of the Spirit is, because **He makes intercession for the saints according to the will of God.***
(Romans 8:27, NKJV, emphasis added)

*And pray in the Spirit on all occasions with all kinds of prayers and requests. With this in mind, be alert and always **keep on praying for all the Lord's people.***
(Ephesians 6:18, NIV, emphasis added)

The paralytic man may have received the miracle, but I can tell you that the four friends who persevered to get him to Jesus were also never the same. Who are you going to put on your speed dial for times of battle? Who will stand with you and agree with you in prayer? Who will boldly take your need to the throne, be led by the Holy Spirit, speak God's Word over your situation, and remain in faith, *no matter what?*

B–R–E–A–T
TRUST IN GOD'S TIMING, BUT NEVER STOP PRAYING

I often wondered why our son suffered and nearly died after he took his first miraculous breath. Why was there an additional battle for his life? When I brought this question to God, I received two answers. First, there are spiritual battles, and second, God's timing of His victory is always perfect.

Let's take a look at the first answer: spiritual warfare. For this, I was directed to the story of Daniel. In his time of need for God's direction and revelation regarding a vision he had of a great conflict, Daniel desperately called out to God in prayer and fasted for three weeks. He then saw an angelic being who told him he was sent immediately in response to Daniel's prayer, but he was caught fighting a spiritual battle with the "prince of the kingdom of Persia," which detained him for 21 days. After the angel delivered the message Daniel had prayed for, he said he had to return to the spiritual battle (Daniel 10:10-14).

There is a warfare in the spiritual realms that affects the natural. One of the groups that prayed for Vaughn reported sensing a battle during their intercessory prayer over Vaughn.

Understanding the spiritual implications of our son's life, after we experienced the recent loss of Chris's dad in the similar manner, I now believe spiritual warfare may have been a factor in our testimony of healing.

However, we can stand strong without fear because we know who the winners are—not only in our story, but in eternity over every spiritual battle: the name above all names, Jesus Christ (Revelation 17:14).

For the second response, God's timing of releasing power for healing was at the exact time it needed to happen.

Delight yourself also in the Lord,
And He shall give you the desires of your heart.
Commit your way *to the Lord,* **Trust** *also in Him, And*
*He shall **bring it to pass**.*
(Psalm 37:4-5, NKJV, emphasis added)

When I look back at how many lives were deeply affected and spiritually strengthened by my son's story, I know God redeemed the time of waiting with His perfect plan of victory. I know the ripples of faith from my son's story would not have existed without the spiritual perseverance of faith in us and others.

For example, had my son been perfect after he took his miraculous breath, my faith would not have been as challenged, and I would not be who I am today. Perhaps I would have attributed his breath to a scientific phenomenon. But seeing his incredibly fast and unexpected recovery not only revealed to us that it was divine intervention, but it also shocked the doctors and everyone who was involved.

Even though we were focused on my son's healing, God was tending to many *other healings* happening at the same time.

"For My thoughts are not your thoughts,
Nor are your ways My ways," says the Lord.
"For as the heavens are higher than the earth,
So are My ways higher than your ways,

And My thoughts than your thoughts."
(Isaiah 55:8-9, NKJV, emphasis added)

Knowing that things are happening in the spiritual realm, as well as God's perfect timing for answers to our prayers, does not mean we should passively wait in our time of need. We are instructed to be persistent in prayer and patient in our times of need while always holding onto hope with joy (Romans 12:12).

I have some planters in front of my house in beautiful, large, shiny blue pots. This summer, they were thriving with vibrant flowers of all colors, including some hot peppers. But after a few weeks in the pots, they were covered in spider webs. I *do not* like spiders. If I see a spider, I shriek until my husband comes to remove it. I was so scared of these webs, I just let them take over until the plants died. This is an example of passive waiting during a difficult time. If we wait because we "trust God" but aren't praying and building our faith during the battle, we may be allowing the enemy to take territory in our hearts over the situation and fear can take over. Instead, God wants us to hope in Him, which is *active*, and He will renew our strength in difficult times (Isaiah 40:31).

Then Jesus told his disciples a parable to show them that
they should always pray and not give up.
(Luke 18:1, NIV, emphasis added)

Continue earnestly in prayer, *being vigilant in it with thanksgiving;*
(Colossians 4:2, NKJV, emphasis added)

B–R–E–A–T–H
HOLD YOUR GROUND
WITH GOD'S WORD

Faith comes by hearing God's Word (Romans 10:17). When we are in trials and our faith is tested, we should dive into God's Word, taking it in regularly for guidance and strength. God's Word is sharper than any two-edged sword (Hebrews 4:12), and the good news of Jesus's victory is the *peace* in our pieces of armor (Ephesians 6:15).

When Vaughn was going through his "no nap, mommy" phase and I knew he was absolutely exhausted, I'd ask if he wanted me to tell a story to help him get sleepy. The story often started excitingly, with a special bright choo-choo train carrying all his favorite toys and food in his very own cable car. Then the story ended with us lying together under a big, beautiful tree, listening to the leaves rustle in the breeze, shaded by the branches, and counting the fruit on the tree, one by one. He would fall fast asleep every time.

There's something so calming about seeing a large, immovable, planted tree. The Bible says this is what we are like when we are full of hope and full of God's Word.

Hope deferred makes the heart sick, but a longing
*fulfilled **is a tree of life.***
(Proverbs 13:12, NIV, emphasis added)

And in His law he meditates day and night.
He shall be like a tree

> ***Planted*** *by the rivers of water,*
> *(Psalm 1:2-3, NKJV, emphasis added)*

> *That they may be called **trees of righteousness**,*
> *The planting of the Lord, that He may be glorified.*
> *(Isaiah 61:3, NKJV, emphasis added)*

When we plant God's Word in us and meditate on it, we become like an immovable tree in our times of battle, with a hope and faith that won't wither away.

> *"It is the Spirit who gives life; the flesh profits nothing.*
> ***The words that I speak to you are spirit, and they are***
> ***life."***
> *(John 6:63, NKJV, emphasis added)*

> *My son, give attention to my words; Incline your ear*
> *to my sayings. Do not let them depart from your eyes;*
> *Keep them in the midst of your heart; **For they are life***
> ***to those who find them, And health to all their flesh.***
> *(Proverbs 4:20-22, NKJV, emphasis added)*

When we remind ourselves through God's Word of His love, protection, promises, and knowledge of who we are in Him, we have the strength to hold on, withstand, and *resist* giving up. God's Word is active and living, and it holds power for every day and every situation.

The Apostle Paul wrote to the Corinthian church about a near-death experience he had during his ministry in Asia. He described that the situation was "far beyond our ability to endure," and he saw his impending brutal death. In other words, the situation not only took his breath away, but he was facing what seemed like a vast mountain of *fear* face-to-face. However, in his letter to the church, he attributed a deliverance that came through resurrected faith and supportive prayer.

*Indeed, we felt we had received the sentence of death. But this happened that **we might not rely on ourselves but on God, who raises the dead.** He has delivered us from such a deadly peril, **and he will deliver us again.** On him we have **set our hope** that he will continue to deliver us, as you help us by your prayers. Then many will give thanks on our behalf for the gracious favor granted us in **answer to the prayers of many.***
(2 Corinthians 1: 9-11, NIV, emphasis added)

I could not have summed up my experience of faith better than Paul did in his letter to Corinth. When we step out of ourselves and our own control, even in the most difficult situations, and instead rely on God's faithfulness and place our hope in His powerful plan for deliverance, we fight the good fight of faith (1 Timothy 6:12).

It stood out to me that Paul mentioned he had hope that God would *continue* to deliver him. His faith was strengthened immensely going through his death-to-breath moment, just like mine. And just like I did, Paul relied on the prayers of his appointed prayer warriors to strengthen his faith and stand in agreement with God's plan over the situation. Paul learned to keep God's breath *no matter what.*

B

Build up your faith in Jesus's Victory

R

Remove the blocks in your relationship with God

E

Embrace every circumstance with praise

A

Appoint faith warriors to battle with you

T

Trust in God's timing, but never stop praying

H

Hold your ground with God's Word

Dear reader, I didn't know what I was going to write when I started this journey of healing, but I can tell you it took me to a place so deep and so profound that I can never return to swimming in the shallow waters of faith.

Deep calls to deep in the roar of your waterfalls; all your waves and breakers have swept over me.
(Psalm 42:7, NIV)

This book is my testimony to the greatness of God, the victory through His Son, Jesus Christ, and His resurrecting power through His Holy Spirit, who lives in us when we accept His grace, purpose, and love into our lives.

My hope and prayer is that the words in this book become a *seed* that you will allow God to plant in your heart so you can see your victory *in* Him, and that we may see His victory come to pass through you.

I believe that God called me by name before the world ever existed, and recorded all of the plans that He had for my days in His book of life (Psalm 139:13-18, Jeremiah 1:5). When you draw close to God, He will draw close to you (James 4:8).

God's wonder-working power is active today, are you ready to keep *His breath?*

LET'S TAKE A BREATH TOGETHER

The following prayers are meant as a guide rather than what you should say word for word. As discussed in Chapter Four, your prayer life is your relationship with God; speak from the heart to your Creator and Sustainer.

Guided Prayer for Salvation

Guided Prayer for Reconciliation

Guided Prayer for Victory

GUIDED PRAYER FOR SALVATION

Dear reader, if you are uncertain that Jesus Christ is your Lord and Savior and you'd like to start living each day with the comfort, power, and love that comes with His Holy Spirit, all it takes is one simple prayer to enter the Kingdom of Heaven. I want to offer the following guided prayer to lead you into salvation and into a relationship with Jesus Christ. As the following is a guided prayer for reference, speak from your heart.

If you declare with your mouth, "Jesus is Lord," and believe in your heart that God raised him from the dead, you will be saved.
(Romans 10:9, NIV)

Dear Heavenly Father, I'm sorry for doing things my way up until now. I want to join your family as your adopted son or daughter and have a personal relationship with You. I am sorry for my sin and believe in my heart that your son, Jesus Christ, died for me to wash away my sin once and for all, that He rose again by the power of your Holy Spirit, and is seated at your right hand until He returns. I not only want to recognize Jesus as my Lord and Savior, but welcome Jesus into my life. Jesus, I receive your Holy Spirit to lead me and help me from this day forward. AMEN.

If you have just prayed this prayer for the first time, there is rejoicing and celebration in heaven over you right now (Luke 15:10)!

GUIDED PRAYER FOR RECONCILIATION

Dear reader, if you have strayed from your faith and let the world turn your heart against God, I'd like to offer you a guided prayer to help you reconcile with your Heavenly Father.

---

*Repent, then, and turn to God, so that your sins may be
wiped out, that times of refreshing may come
from the Lord,*
(Acts 3:19, NIV)

Dear Heavenly Father, I need your help to renew my faith and remove my doubt. Jesus, please show me the blocks I have let come between my relationship with you, and please forgive me and help me remove them. Holy Spirit, I am sorry for ignoring your voice and hindering your power in my life by putting my wants before God's. I welcome your breath into my life and renew my spirit right now.

As I draw closer to you, LORD, I look forward to experiencing you drawing closer to me. Help me hear your voice again, and I welcome all of the guidance, plans, blessings, and future that you have in store for me from this day forward. I thank you for always being there, waiting for me to return. In Jesus's name AMEN.

GUIDED PRAYER FOR VICTORY

My heart goes out to everyone facing a major battle in their life right now. Now more than ever, the world is crying out for the great *Comforter*. Let's raise our shields of faith through prayer together. Remember this: Jesus intercedes and is your advocate; His Holy Spirit dwells in you and guides you; and God the Father cares more about you than you can ever imagine. With that in mind, let's pray!

---

but those who hope in the LORD will renew their strength. They will soar on wings like eagles; they will run and not grow weary, they will walk and not be faint.
(Isaiah 40:31, NIV)

Today, I stand on the promises God has for my life. I bind the work of the enemy over [my situation] and believe in the power and victory that Jesus did in the work at the cross. I declare the powerful name of Jesus over [my situation]. Heavenly Father, your ways are higher than my ways, and your thoughts are higher than my thoughts. Let me rise above my situation and soar with wings like eagles to see the greater view that you have for me in this difficult time. Thank you for your power, love, comfort, and guidance right now. Let me hear your voice over [my situation], not the enemy's. Fear must leave me now in Jesus's name! Jesus, fill me with your peace which surpasses all human understanding and lead me with clarity to your path to prosper me and not to harm me, your path that gives me hope and a future. Thank you for your faithfulness. Help me remove my doubt so I may stand firm in my hope and perfect my faith in You. I'm standing now like an immovable tree rooted in Your promises and Word. Send me warriors in my path who will stand in agreement with me and align me with your will. Holy Spirit, give me the wisdom I need to overcome, lead me to pray over my situation, and help me stay in Your perfect peace. In the victorious name of Jesus! Amen.

WHAT QUESTIONS WOULD YOU LIKE TO ASK GOD?

WRITE ANY BLOCKS THAT MAY BE SPIRITUAL BARRIERS IN YOUR LIFE

EXPLORE A LIST OF YOUR APPOINTED PRAYER WARRIORS

____
____
____
____
____
____
____
____
____
____
____
____
____
____
____
____
____
____

WRITE YOUR OWN PRAYERS
OF VICTORY

THE RESEARCH: BIBLIOGRAPHY

1. Christie, H., Hamilton-Giachritsis, C., McGuire, R. et al. "Exploring the Perceived Impact of Parental PTSD on Parents and Parenting Behaviours—A Qualitative Study." *J Child Fam Stud* 32, 3378–3388 (2023). https://doi.org/10.1007/s10826-023-02614-z

2. "Benefits of Hypothermia for Infants Continue through Early Childhood." *National Institute of Child Health and Human Development (NICHD)*, press release, May 30, 2012. Accessed January 4, 2026. https://www.nichd.nih.gov/newsroom/releases/053012-newborn-hypothermia

3. Tagin MA, Woolcott CG, Vincer MJ, Whyte RK, Stinson DA. "Hypothermia for Neonatal Hypoxic Ischemic Encephalopathy: An Updated Systematic Review and Meta-analysis." *Arch Pediatr Adolesc Med.* 2012;166(6):558–566. https://doi.org/10.1001/archpediatrics.2011.1772

4. Edwards A D, Brocklehurst P, Gunn A J, Halliday H, Juszczak E, Levene M et al. "Neurological outcomes at 18 months of age after moderate hypothermia for perinatal hypoxic ischaemic encephalopathy: synthesis and meta-analysis of trial data." *BMJ* 2010; 340 :c363 https://doi.org/10.1136/bmj.c363

5. Kapadia VS, Wyckoff MH. "Epinephrine Use during Newborn Resuscitation." *Frontiers in Pediatrics.* 2017;5:97. https://doi.org/10.3389/fped.2017.00097

6. "The Lazarus Effect (Phenomenon)." Cleveland Clinic. Medically reviewed article. Accessed March 17, 2026. https://my.clevelandclinic.org/health/articles/24876-lazarus-effect

7. Mullen, Stephen MB, BAO, BCH; Roberts, Zöe MBBS, MRCPCH; Tuthill, David MB, BCh, FRCPCH; Owens, Laura MBBCh, MRCEM; Te Water Naude, Johann; Maguire, Sabine MBBCh, MRCPI, FRCPCH. "Lazarus Syndrome — Challenges Created by Pediatric Autoresuscitation." *Pediatric Emergency Care* 37(4):p e210-e211, April 2021. https://doi.org/10.1097/pec.0000000000001593

8. Elizabeth E. Foglia, Gary Weiner, Maria Fernanda B. de Almeida, Jonathan Wyllie, Myra H. Wyckoff, Yacov Rabi, Ruth Guinsburg, INTERNATIONAL LIAISON COMMITTEE ON RESUSCITATION NEONATAL LIFE SUPPORT TASK FORCE; "Duration of Resuscitation at Birth, Mortality, and Neurodevelopment: A Systematic Review." *Pediatrics* September 2020; 146 (3): e20201449. https://doi.org/10.1542/peds.2020-1449

9. Sankaran, D., Lee, H.C., Park, L. et al. "Risk factors, incidence, and outcomes of neonatal respiratory extracorporeal membrane oxygenation including association with therapeutic hypothermia in California during 2013–2020." *J Perinatol* 44, 1442–1447 (2024). https://doi.org/10.1038/s41372-024-02067-2

10. Christoph P. Hornik, Eric M. Graham, Kevin Hill, Jennifer S. Li, George Ofori-Amanfo, Reese H. Clark, P. Brian Smith. "Cardiopulmonary resuscitation in hospitalized infants." *Early Human Development.* Volume 101, (2016):p 17-22. https://doi.org/10.1016/j.earlhumdev.2016.03.015

11. Boyle, Katharine MD; Felling, Ryan MD, PhD; Yiu, Alvin BS; Battarjee, Wejdan MD; Schwartz, Jamie McElrath MD; Salorio, Cynthia PhD; Bembea, Melania M. MD, MPH, PhD. "Neurologic Outcomes After Extracorporeal Membrane Oxygenation: A Systematic Review." *Pediatric Critical Care Medicine* 19(8):p 760-766, August 2018. https://doi.org/10.1097/PCC.0000000000001612

12. Chalak LF, Pappas A, Tan S, et al. "Association Between Increased Seizures During Rewarming After Hypothermia for Neonatal Hypoxic Ischemic Encephalopathy and Abnormal Neurodevelopmental Outcomes at 2-Year Follow-up: A Nested Multisite Cohort Study." *JAMA Neurol.* 2021;78(12):1484–1493. https://doi.org/10.1001/jamaneurol.2021.3723

13. Kimberly A. Allen, Debra H. Brandon. "Hypoxic Ischemic Encephalopathy: Pathophysiology and Experimental Treatments." *Newborn and Infant Nursing Reviews.* Volume 11, Issue 3, 2011: P 125-133. https://doi.org/10.1053/j.nainr.2011.07.004

14. Strong's Greek Lexicon (G4335). *proseuchē.* BibleStudyTools.com. Accessed January 4, 2026.
https://www.biblestudytools.com/lexicons/greek/kjv/proseuche.html

15. Strong's Greek Lexicon (G2666). *katapiein.* BibleHub.com. Accessed March 21, 2026.
https://biblehub.com/greek/katapiein_2666.htm

16. Strong's Greek Lexicon (G5293). *hupotassō.* BibleStudyTools.com. Accessed January 4, 2026.
https://www.biblestudytools.com/lexicons/greek/kjv/hupotasso.html

17. Strong's Greek Lexicon (G436). *anthistēmi.* BibleHub.com. Accessed January 4, 2026.
https://biblehub.com/strongs/greek/436.htm

18. Strong's Hebrew Lexicon (H7307). *ruach.* BibleHub.com. Accessed January 6, 2026.
https://biblehub.com/strongs/hebrew/7307.htm

19. Strong's Greek Lexicon (G4570). *sbennumi.* BibleTools.org. Accessed January 4, 2026.
https://www.bibletools.org/index.cfm/fuseaction/Lexicon.show/ID/G4570/sbennumi.htm

20. Strong's Hebrew Lexicon. *rapha.* BibleStudyTools.com. Accessed January 4, 2026.
https://www.biblestudytools.com/lexicons/hebrew/nas/rapha.html

21. National Park Service. "Traveling Trunk Additional Activities: Civil War Music." *Gettysburg National Military Park, Pennsylvania.* Accessed March 21, 2026.
https://www.nps.gov/gett/learn/education/a-nation-at-war-traveling-trunk-additional-activities-civil-war-music.htm

Visit the author's website for more information and directions on how to submit a review. Your positive review will help the book reach a wider audience.

KellyMaureen.Faith